Basic Line

GRAPHING

Skills

Practice Workbook

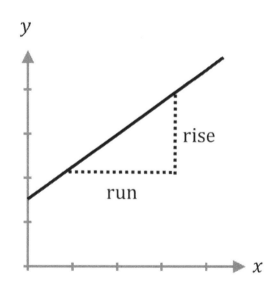

Improve Your Math Fluency Series

Chris McMullen, Ph.D.

Basic Linear Graphing Skills Practice Workbook

Plotting Points, Straight Lines, Slope, y-Intercept & More

Improve Your Math Fluency Series

Copyright © 2015 Chris McMullen, Ph.D.

Zishka Publishing

Professional & Technical > Science > Mathematics > Graphs
Education > Specific Skills > Mathematics > Graphs

ISBN-10: 1-941691-05-6
EAN-13: 978-1-941691-05-2

Contents

Making the Most of this Workbook

Mathematics is a language. You can't hold a decent conversation in any language if you have a limited vocabulary or if you are not fluent. In order to become successful in mathematics, you need to practice until you have mastered the fundamentals and developed fluency in the subject. This workbook will help you improve your fluency with basic graphing skills.

This workbook covers the following topics:
- reading (x, y) coordinates
- plotting points on a graph
- finding the slope of a straight line
- finding the y-intercept
- the equation for a straight line

Each chapter begins with a concise explanation of the concepts along with examples. Use the examples as a guide until you become fluent in the technique.

After you complete a page, check your answers with the answer key in the back of the book. Practice makes permanent, but not necessarily perfect: If you practice making mistakes, you will learn your mistakes. Check your answers and learn from your mistakes such that you practice solving the problems correctly. This way your practice will make perfect.

Chapter 0

Basic Graphing Terminology

Concepts

A graph features a **coordinate system**.

The standard **Cartesian** coordinate system includes two coordinates, x and y. The x-axis is horizontal, while the y-axis is vertical (see the illustration below).

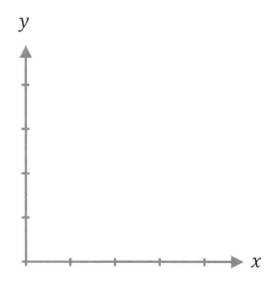

Every point on a graph is assigned an **ordered pair**, designated as (x, y). The value of x is called the **abscissa**, while the value of y is called the **ordinate**.

In an **ordered pair** (x, y), the value of x is a horizontal measure and the value of y is a vertical measure (see the illustration that follows).

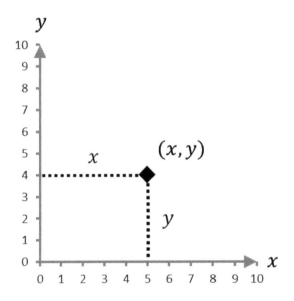

The x- and y-axes meet at the **origin**.[1] The (x, y) coordinates of the origin are $(0, 0)$. In the graph shown above, the origin appears at the bottom left corner. The point marked in the graph is $(5, 4)$.

Each axis includes tick marks and a numerical scale to help you read values from the graph. When it's necessary to read between the lines, this process is called **interpolation**.

---

[1] The word axis is singular, while the word axes is plural. For example, we refer to the x-axis, which is just one axis, or we refer to the x- and y-axes, which are two different axes.

The x- and y-axes divide the coordinate system into four distinct regions called **Quadrants**.

The Quadrants are labeled as follows:
- Quadrant I is at the top right.
- Quadrant II is at the top left.
- Quadrant III is at the bottom left.
- Quadrant IV is at the bottom right.

This order is counterclockwise, as illustrated below.

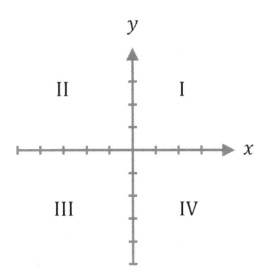

The x- and y-coordinates can each be **positive** or **negative**:
- x is positive when the point is right of the origin.
- x is negative when the point is left of the origin.
- y is positive when the point is above the origin.
- y is negative when the point is below the origin.

Here is a breakdown of the **signs** by Quadrant:
- In Quadrant I, both x and y are positive.
- In Quadrant II, x is negative while y is positive.
- In Quadrant III, both x and y are negative.
- In Quadrant IV, x is positive while y is negative.

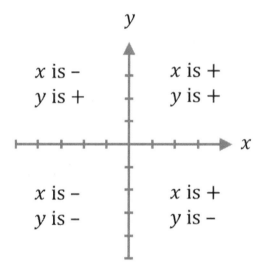

The **slope** of a line tells you how steep it is. The greater the slope, the steeper the line. A horizontal line has zero slope.

The **slope** of a line equals rise over run:

$$slope = \frac{rise}{run}$$

The **rise** is the vertical separation between two points, whereas the **run** is the horizontal separation between two points.

Slope can be positive or negative:
- A line with positive slope angles up to the right.
- A line with negative slope angles down to the right.
- A line with zero slope is horizontal.

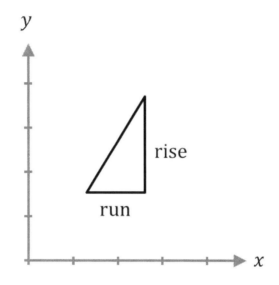

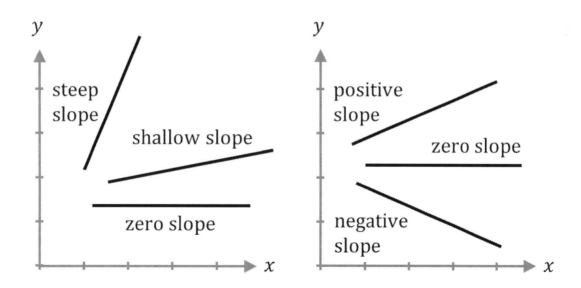

A line intersects the y-axis at the **y-intercept**. This is the value of y for which x equals 0.

The equation for a straight line is:

$$y = mx + b$$

In this equation:
- m represents the slope
- b represents the y-intercept

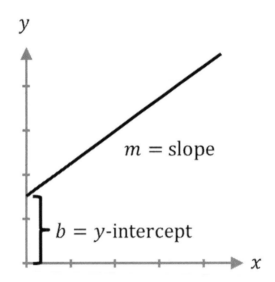

Chapter 1

Read (x, y) Coordinates in Quadrant I

Concepts

Any point on a graph can be specified with an ordered pair of the form (x, y). The point $(0, 0)$ is called the origin.

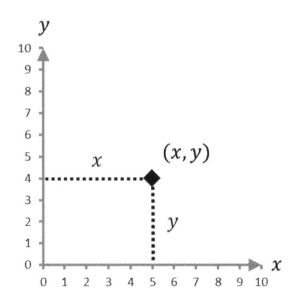

- The value of x is the horizontal distance from the origin. Go right from the origin to find x.
- The value of y is the vertical distance from the origin. Go up from the origin to find y.
- The (x, y) coordinates of the point shown above are $(5, 4)$.

Examples

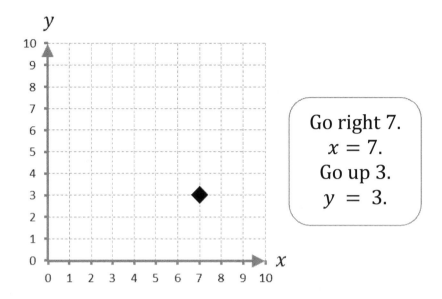

Ex. 1. The (x, y) coordinates of the point above are $(7, 3)$.

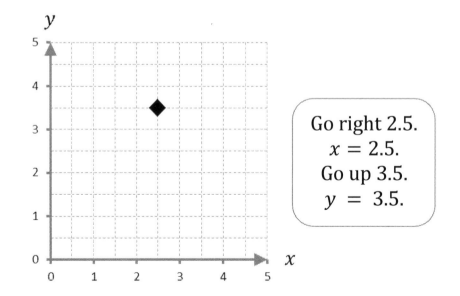

Ex. 2. The (x, y) coordinates of the point above are $(2.5, 3.5)$.

Basic Linear Graphing Skills

Give the (x, y) coordinates of each point graphed below.

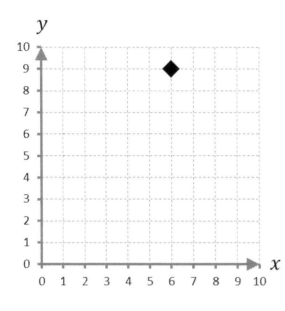

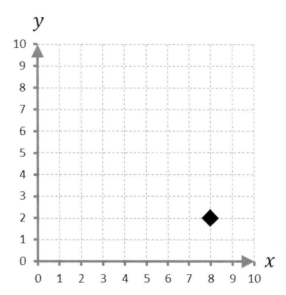

#1. $(x, y) =$ _____

#2. $(x, y) =$ _____

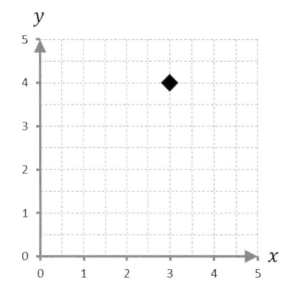

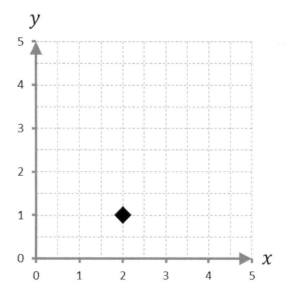

#3. $(x, y) =$ _____

#4. $(x, y) =$ _____

Give the (x, y) coordinates of each point graphed below.

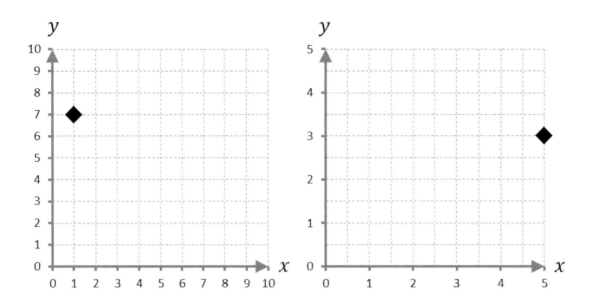

#5. $(x, y) =$ _____   #6. $(x, y) =$ _____

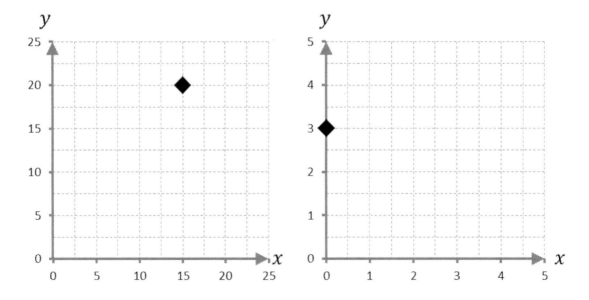

#7. $(x, y) =$ _____   #8. $(x, y) =$ _____

Basic Linear Graphing Skills

Give the (x, y) coordinates of each point graphed below.

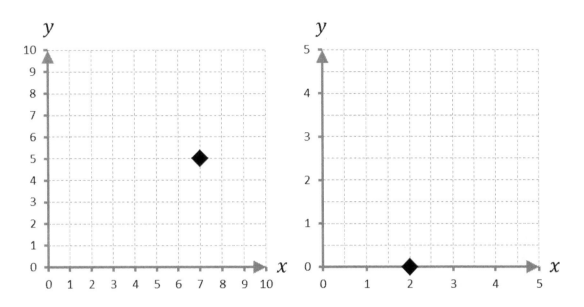

#9. $(x, y) =$ _____

#10. $(x, y) =$ _____

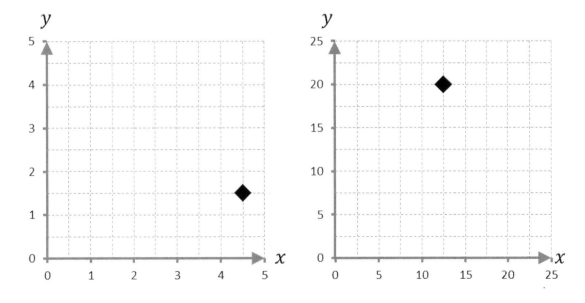

#11. $(x, y) =$ _____

#12. $(x, y) =$ _____

Give the (x, y) coordinates of each point graphed below.

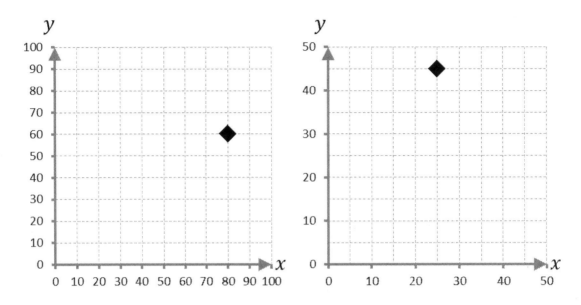

#13. $(x, y) =$ _____   #14. $(x, y) =$ _____

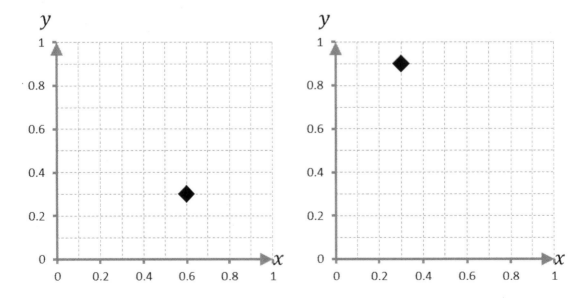

#15. $(x, y) =$ _____   #16. $(x, y) =$ _____

Chapter 2

Read (x, y) Coordinates in Quadrants I-IV

Concepts

The x- and y-coordinates can each by positive or negative.
- x is positive when the point is right of the origin.
- x is negative when the point is left of the origin.
- y is positive when the point is above the origin.
- y is negative when the point is below the origin.

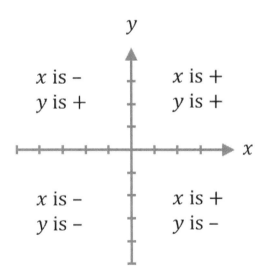

Examples

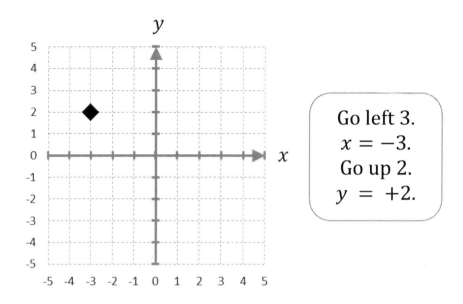

Ex. 1. The (x, y) coordinates of the point above are (−3, 2).

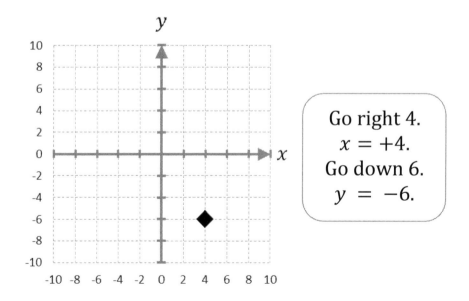

Ex. 2. The (x, y) coordinates of the point above are (4, −6).

Basic Linear Graphing Skills

Give the (x, y) coordinates of each point graphed below.

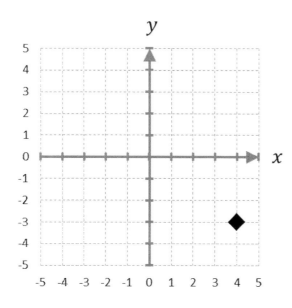

#1. $(x, y) =$ _____

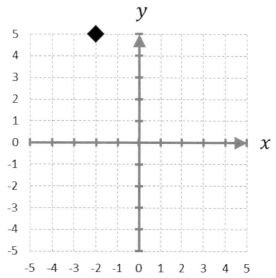

#2. $(x, y) =$ _____

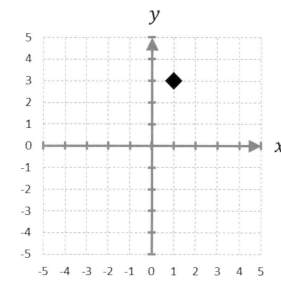

#3. $(x, y) =$ _____

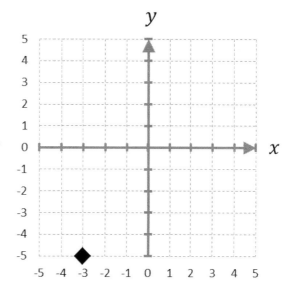

#4. $(x, y) =$ _____

Give the (x, y) coordinates of each point graphed below.

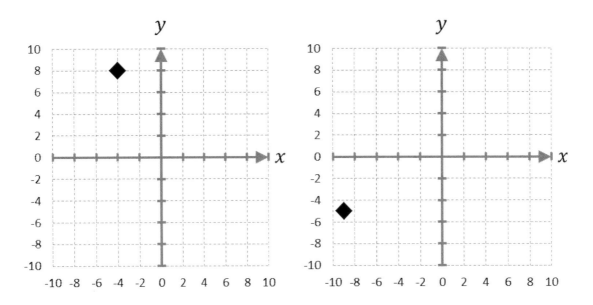

#5. $(x, y) =$ _____

#6. $(x, y) =$ _____

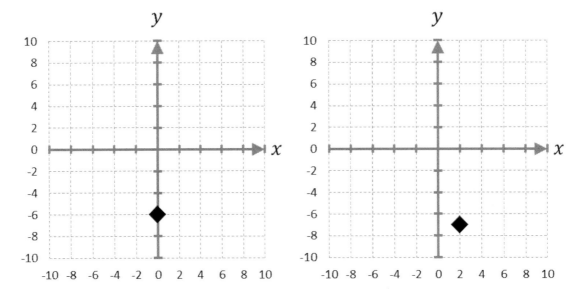

#7. $(x, y) =$ _____

#8. $(x, y) =$ _____

Give the (x, y) coordinates of each point graphed below.

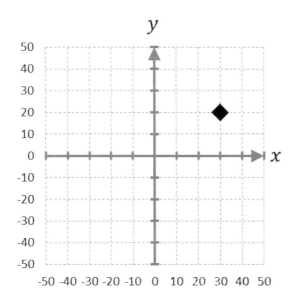

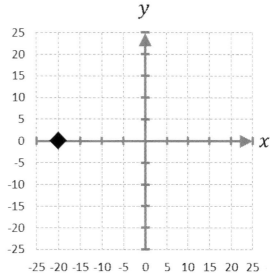

#9. $(x, y) =$ _____

#10. $(x, y) =$ _____

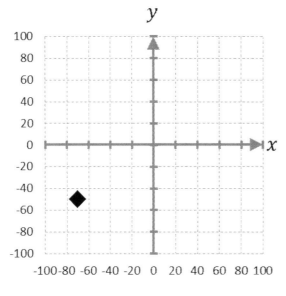

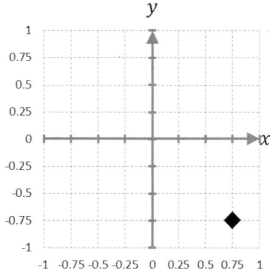

#11. $(x, y) =$ _____

#12. $(x, y) =$ _____

Give the (x, y) coordinates of each point graphed below.

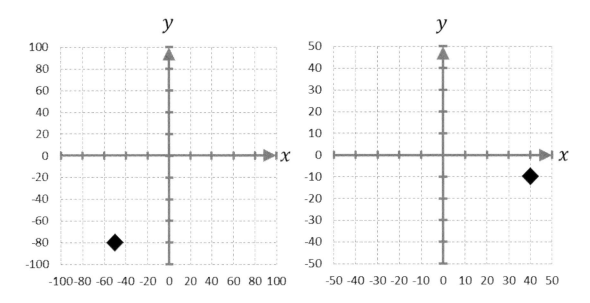

#13. $(x, y) = $ _____

#14. $(x, y) = $ _____

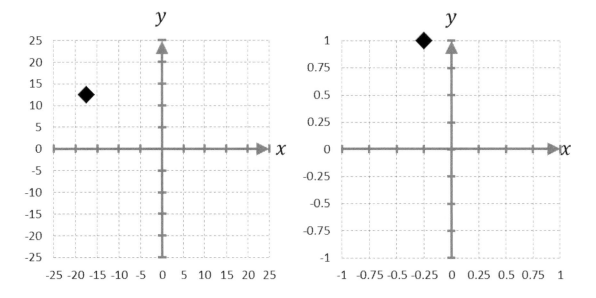

#15. $(x, y) = $ _____

#16. $(x, y) = $ _____

Chapter 3

Plot Points in Quadrant I

Concepts

Any point on a graph can be specified with an ordered pair of the form (x, y). The point $(0, 0)$ is called the origin.

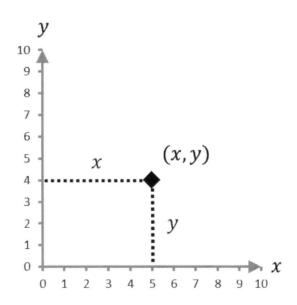

- The value of x is the horizontal distance from the origin. Go right from the origin to find x.
- The value of y is the vertical distance from the origin. Go up from the origin to find y.
- The (x, y) coordinates of the point shown above are $(5, 4)$.

Examples

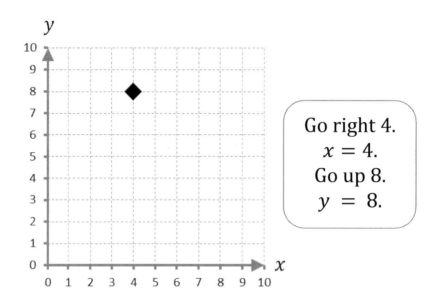

Go right 4.
$x = 4$.
Go up 8.
$y = 8$.

Ex. 1. The (x, y) coordinates of the point above are $(4, 8)$.

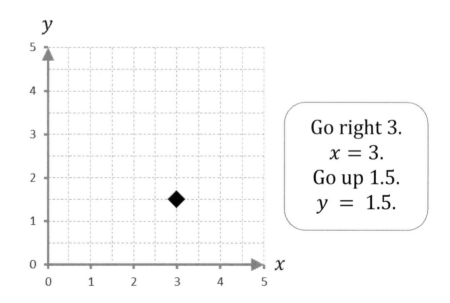

Go right 3.
$x = 3$.
Go up 1.5.
$y = 1.5$.

Ex. 2. The (x, y) coordinates of the point above are $(3, 1.5)$.

Graph each point according to the (x, y) coordinates given.

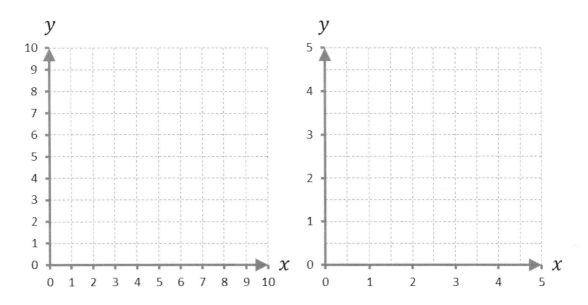

#1. $(x, y) = (9, 5)$

#2. $(x, y) = (1, 4)$

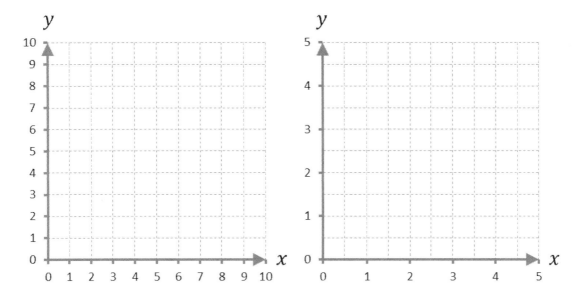

#3. $(x, y) = (3, 6)$

#4. $(x, y) = (3, 5)$

Graph each point according to the (x, y) coordinates given.

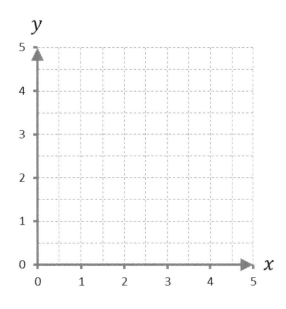

#5. $(x, y) = (2, 0)$

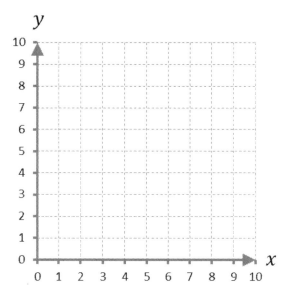

#6. $(x, y) = (6, 2)$

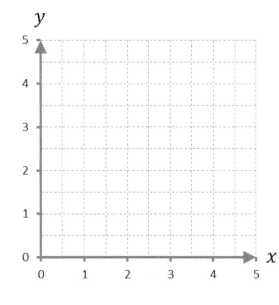

#7. $(x, y) = (1, 5)$

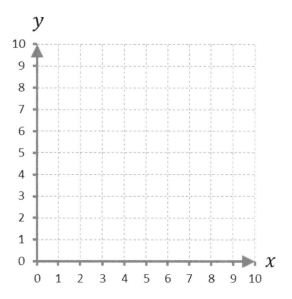

#8. $(x, y) = (7, 9)$

Basic Linear Graphing Skills

Graph each point according to the (x, y) coordinates given.

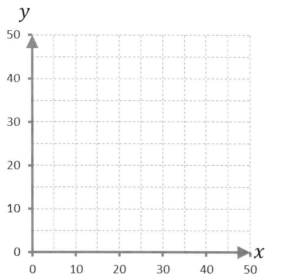

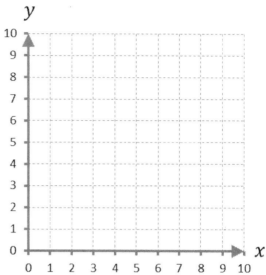

#9. $(x, y) = (40, 15)$ #10. $(x, y) = (0, 8)$

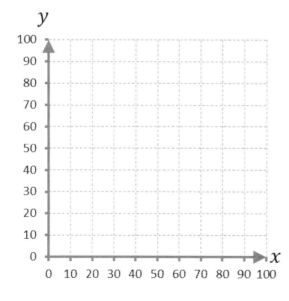

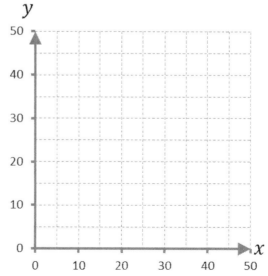

#11. $(x, y) = (20, 70)$ #12. $(x, y) = (20, 15)$

x 27 y

Graph each point according to the (x, y) coordinates given.

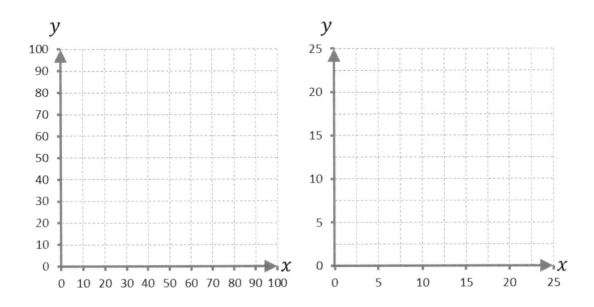

#13. $(x, y) = (70, 90)$

#14. $(x, y) = (22.5, 2.5)$

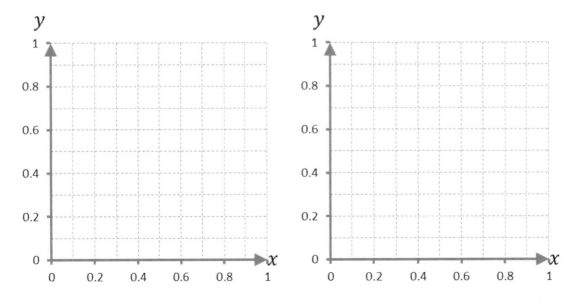

#15. $(x, y) = (0.7, 0.4)$

#16. $(x, y) = (0.3, 0.5)$

Chapter 4

Plot Points in Quadrants I-IV

Concepts

The x- and y-coordinates can each by positive or negative.
- x is positive when the point is right of the origin.
- x is negative when the point is left of the origin.
- y is positive when the point is above the origin.
- y is negative when the point is below the origin.

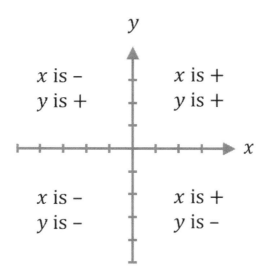

Examples

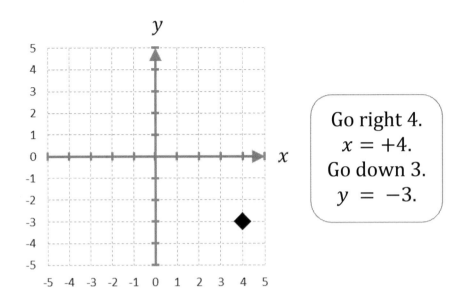

Ex. 1. The (x, y) coordinates of the point above are (4, –3).

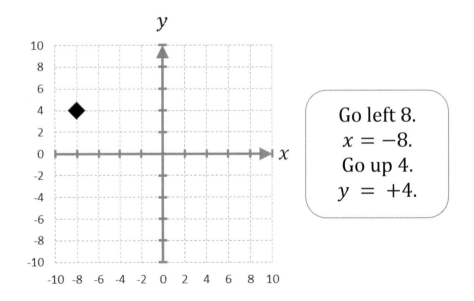

Ex. 2. The (x, y) coordinates of the point above are (–8, 4).

Graph each point according to the (x, y) coordinates given.

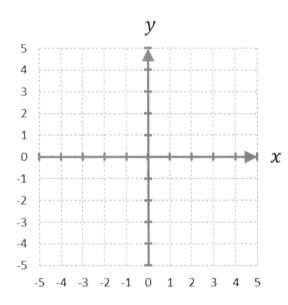

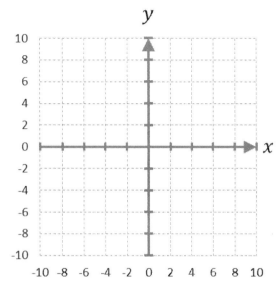

#1. $(x, y) = (-2, -4)$

#2. $(x, y) = (-6, 8)$

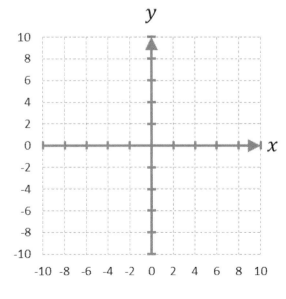

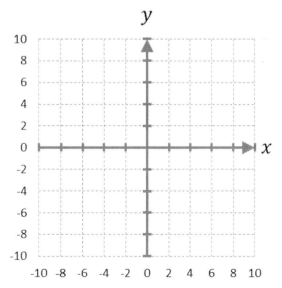

#3. $(x, y) = (2, 8)$

#4. $(x, y) = (4, -10)$

Graph each point according to the (x, y) coordinates given.

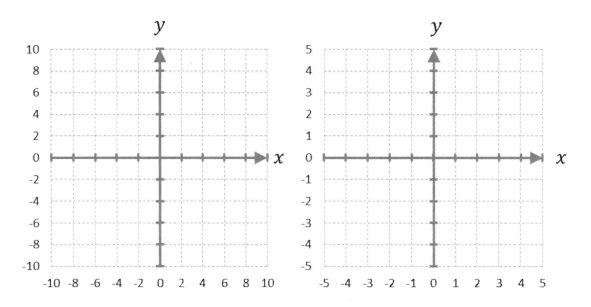

#5. $(x, y) = (9, -3)$

#6. $(x, y) = (-1, 3)$

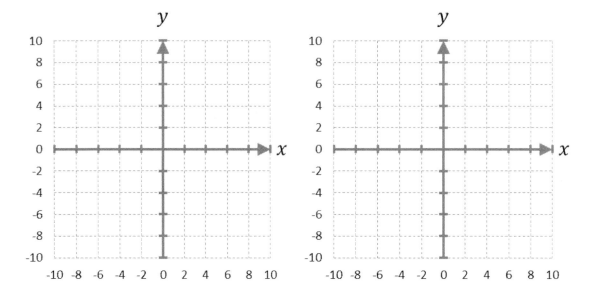

#7. $(x, y) = (-4, -7)$

#8. $(x, y) = (0, -6)$

Graph each point according to the (x, y) coordinates given.

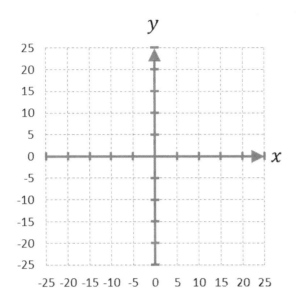

#9. $(x, y) = (-20, 10)$

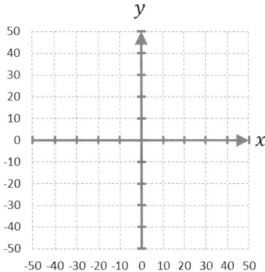

#10. $(x, y) = (35, 35)$

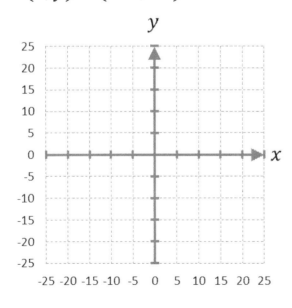

#11. $(x, y) = (-15, 0)$

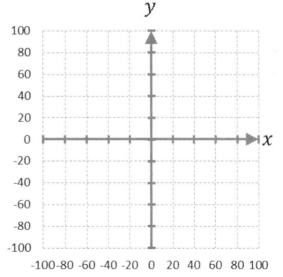

#12. $(x, y) = (-90, 60)$

Graph each point according to the (x, y) coordinates given.

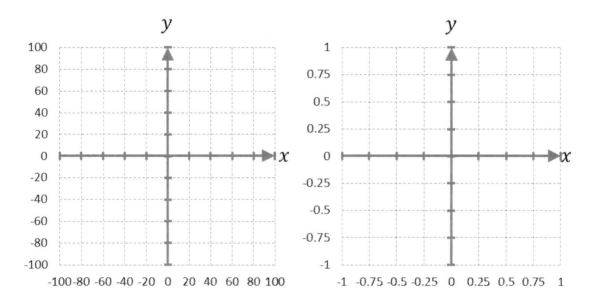

#13. $(x, y) = (-20, 90)$ #14. $(x, y) = (-0.75, -0.25)$

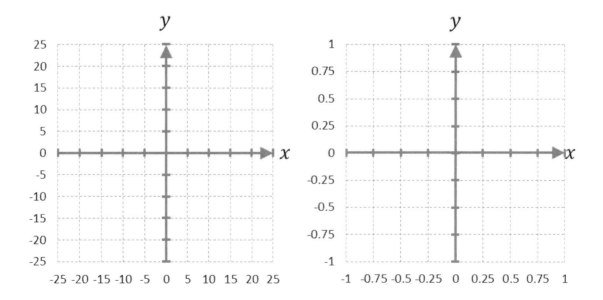

#15. $(x, y) = (12.5, -7.5)$ #16. $(x, y) = (-0.25, 0.5)$

Chapter 5

Find the Slope Given Two Points

Concepts

The slope of a line tells you how steep it is.
- A line with more slope is steep.
- The greater the slope, the steeper the line
- A line with less slope is shallow (not steep).
- A horizontal line has zero slope.

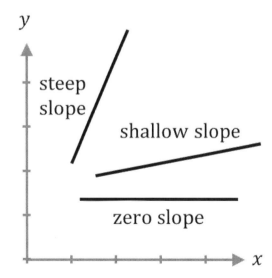

Slope can be positive or negative:
- A line with positive slope angles up to the right.
- A line with negative slope angles down to the right.
- A line with zero slope is horizontal.

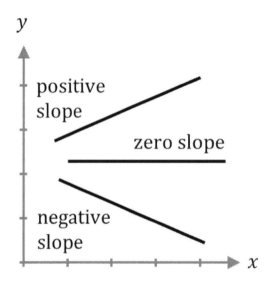

The **slope** of a line equals rise over run:

$$slope = \frac{rise}{run}$$

Rise and run are defined as follows:
- The rise is the vertical separation between 2 points.
- The run is the horizontal separation between 2 points.

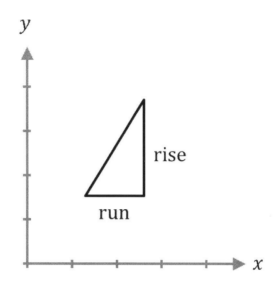

Given the coordinates of two points, (x_1, y_1) and (x_2, y_2), the slope of the line joining these points can be found as follows:

- $rise = y_2 - y_1$
- $run = x_2 - x_1$
- $slope = \dfrac{rise}{run}$

Combining these steps results in the following handy formula:

$$slope = \frac{y_2 - y_1}{x_2 - x_1}$$

Examples

Ex. 1. Find the slope of a line passing through the following points:

$$(1, 2) \text{ and } (3, 8)$$

Identify the values of x_1, y_1, x_2, and y_2:
- $x_1 = 1$
- $y_1 = 2$
- $x_2 = 3$
- $y_2 = 8$

Plug these values into the slope formula:

$$slope = \frac{y_2 - y_1}{x_2 - x_1} = \frac{8 - 2}{3 - 1} = \frac{6}{2} = 3$$

Ex. 2. Find the slope of a line passing through the following points:

$$(-5, -2) \text{ and } (-2, 1)$$

Identify the values of x_1, y_1, x_2, and y_2:
- $x_1 = -5$
- $y_1 = -2$
- $x_2 = -2$
- $y_2 = 1$

Two minuses make a plus.

Plug these values into the slope formula:

$$slope = \frac{y_2 - y_1}{x_2 - x_1} = \frac{1 - (-2)}{-2 - (-5)} = \frac{1 + 2}{-2 + 5} = \frac{3}{3} = 1$$

Find the slope of a line passing through each pair of points.

#1. (3, 1) and (7, 9)

#2. (2, 4) and (5, 22)

Find the slope of a line passing through each pair of points.

#3. (–2, –2) and (3, 3)

#4. (2, 7) and (5, 7)

Find the slope of a line passing through each pair of points.

#5. (1, −1) and (5, 15)

#6. (6, 8) and (9, 2)

Find the slope of a line passing through each pair of points.

#7. (0, –3) and (3, 9)

#8. (–1, –9) and (3, –1)

Find the slope of a line passing through each pair of points.

#9. (–7, 6) and (–4, –9)

#10. (–4, 0) and (0, 12)

Find the slope of a line passing through each pair of points.

#11. (5, 10) and (8, –2)

#12. (2, 5) and (3, –4)

Find the slope of a line passing through each pair of points.

#13. (−4, 1) and (−1, 25)

#14. (−9, −9) and (−1, 7)

Find the slope of a line passing through each pair of points.

#15. (–2, 9) and (2, 1)

#16. (–8, –2) and (–6, –8)

Chapter 6

Find the Slope of a Line

Concepts

Given the graph of a straight line, you can find its slope with two easy steps:

- First, read the (x, y) coordinates of two points on the line.
- Next, use the technique from Chapter 5 to find the slope.

Choose the two points wisely:

- It should be easy to read both x and y.
- The two points should be far apart (to reduce error).
- Both points must lie on the line.

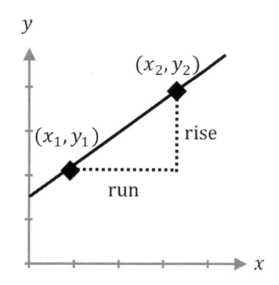

Examples

Ex. 1. Find the slope of the line shown in the graph.

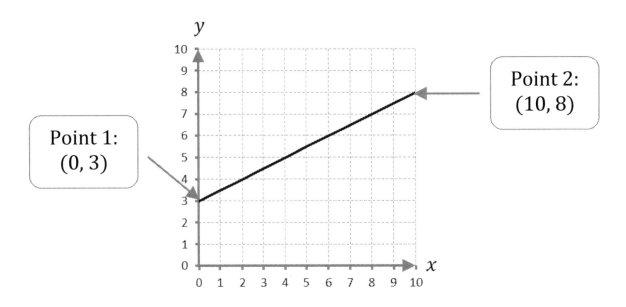

Read the (x, y) coordinates of two different points on the line:

- $(x_1, y_1) = (0, 3)$
- $(x_2, y_2) = (10, 8)$

Plug these points into the slope formula from Chapter 5:

$$slope = \frac{y_2 - y_1}{x_2 - x_1} = \frac{8 - 3}{10 - 0} = \frac{5}{10} = \frac{1}{2} = 0.5$$

Ex. 2. Find the slope of the line shown in the graph.

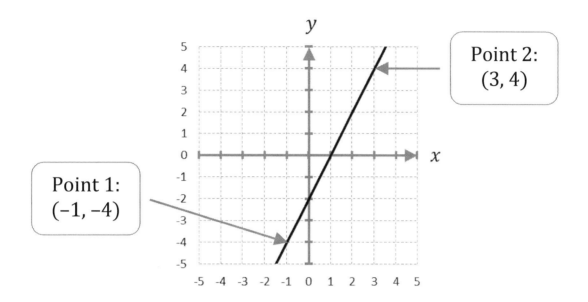

Read the (x, y) coordinates of two different points on the line:
- $(x_1, y_1) = (-1, -4)$
- $(x_2, y_2) = (3, 4)$

Plug these points into the slope formula from Chapter 5:

$$slope = \frac{y_2 - y_1}{x_2 - x_1} = \frac{4 - (-4)}{3 - (-1)} = \frac{4 + 4}{3 + 1} = \frac{8}{4} = 2$$

(Remember, two minuses make a plus.)

#1. Find the slope of the line shown in the graph.

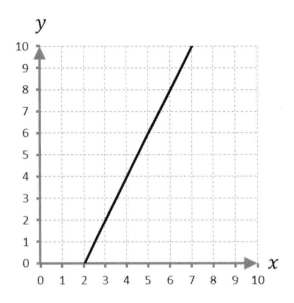

Mark the two points above that you are using to find the slope.

Show your work here:

Final answer = _____

#2. Find the slope of the line shown in the graph.

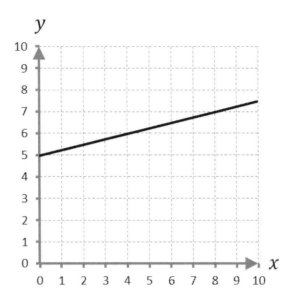

Mark the two points above that you are using to find the slope.

Show your work here:

Final answer = _____

#3. Find the slope of the line shown in the graph.

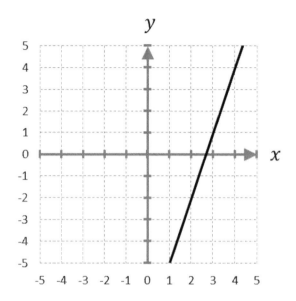

Mark the two points above that you are using to find the slope.

Show your work here:

Final answer = _____

#4. Find the slope of the line shown in the graph.

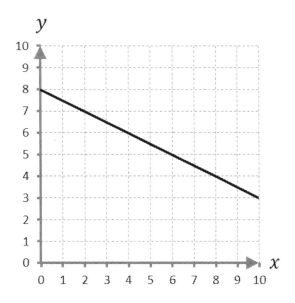

Mark the two points above that you are using to find the slope.

Show your work here:

Final answer = _____

#5. Find the slope of the line shown in the graph.

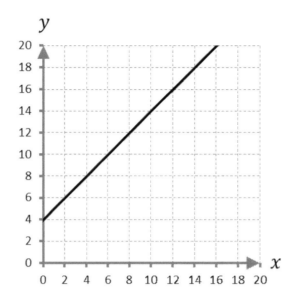

Mark the two points above that you are using to find the slope.

Show your work here:

Final answer = _____

#6. Find the slope of the line shown in the graph.

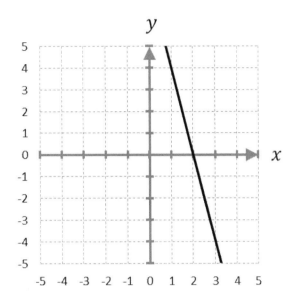

Mark the two points above that you are using to find the slope.

Show your work here:

Final answer = _____

#7. Find the slope of the line shown in the graph.

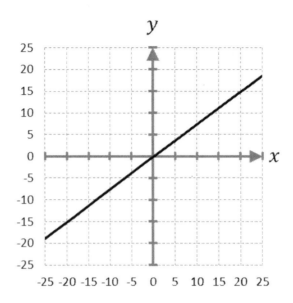

Mark the two points above that you are using to find the slope.

Show your work here:

Final answer = _____

#8. Find the slope of the line shown in the graph.

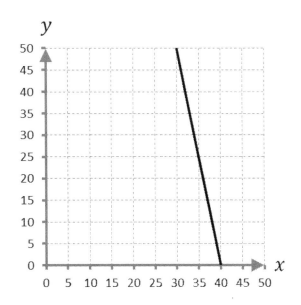

Mark the two points above that you are using to find the slope.

Show your work here:

Final answer = _____

#9. Find the slope of the line shown in the graph.

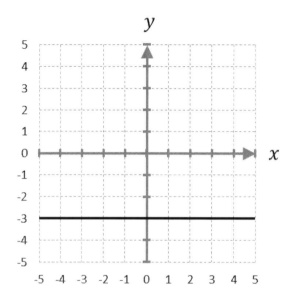

Mark the two points above that you are using to find the slope.

Show your work here:

Final answer = _____

#10. Find the slope of the line shown in the graph.

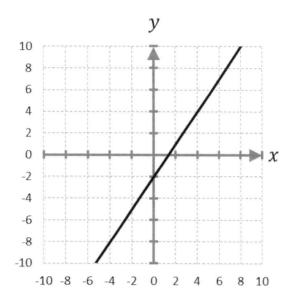

Mark the two points above that you are using to find the slope.

Show your work here:

Final answer = _____

#11. Find the slope of the line shown in the graph.

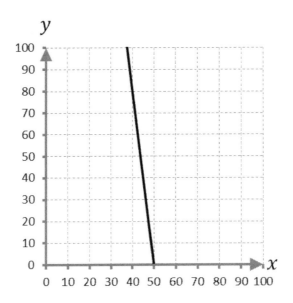

Mark the two points above that you are using to find the slope.

Show your work here:

Final answer = _____

#12. Find the slope of the line shown in the graph.

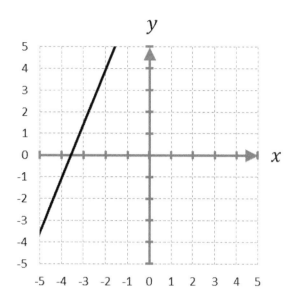

Mark the two points above that you are using to find the slope.

Show your work here:

Final answer = _____

#13. Find the slope of the line shown in the graph.

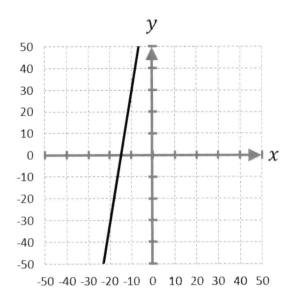

Mark the two points above that you are using to find the slope.

Show your work here:

Final answer = _____

#14. Find the slope of the line shown in the graph.

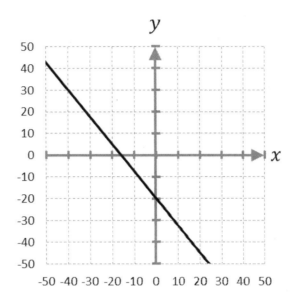

Mark the two points above that you are using to find the slope.

Show your work here:

Final answer = _____

#15. Find the slope of the line shown in the graph.

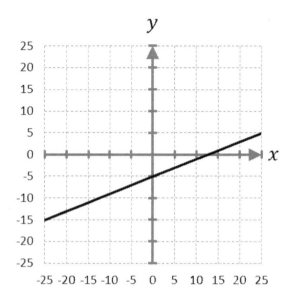

Mark the two points above that you are using to find the slope.

Show your work here:

Final answer = _____

Chapter 7

Determine the *y*-Intercept

Concepts

A line intersects the *y*-axis at the *y*-intercept.

To find the *y*-intercept, answer one of these two questions. (It doesn't matter which one, as the two questions are equivalent.)
- What is the value of *y* where the line crosses the *y*-axis?
- What is the value of *y* when *x* equals zero?

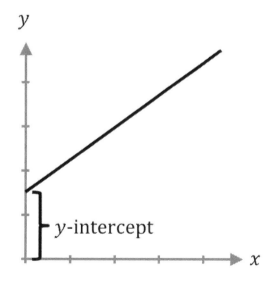

Examples

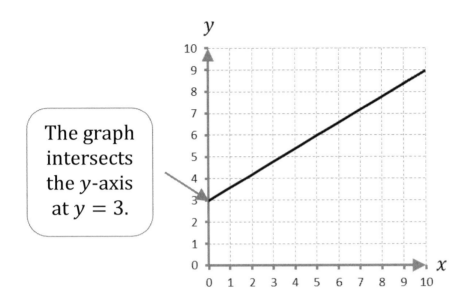

The graph intersects the y-axis at $y = 3$.

Ex. 1. The y-intercept is 3.

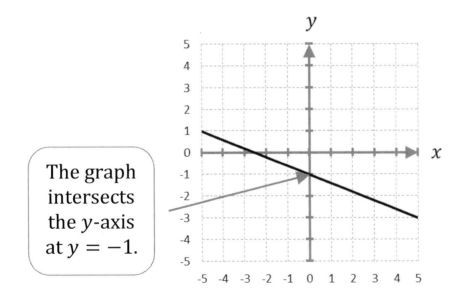

The graph intersects the y-axis at $y = -1$.

Ex. 2. The y-intercept is –1.

Determine the y-intercept of each line.

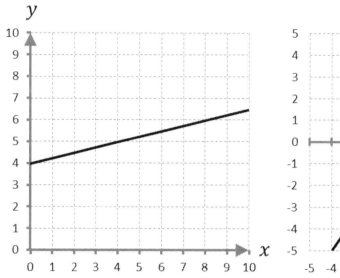 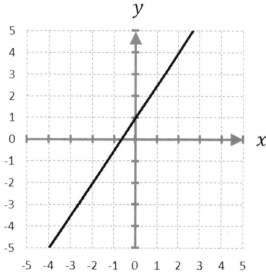

#1. y-intercept = _____   #2. y-intercept = _____

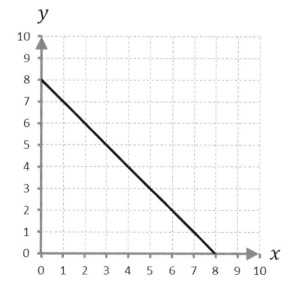 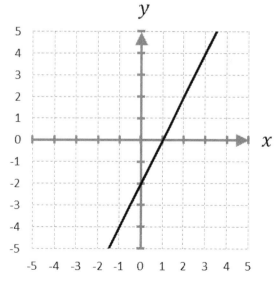

#3. y intercept − _____   #4. y-intercept = _____

Determine the y-intercept of each line.

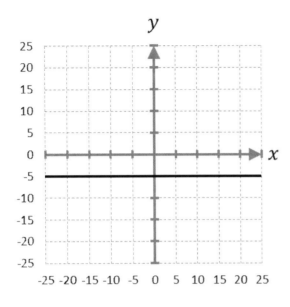

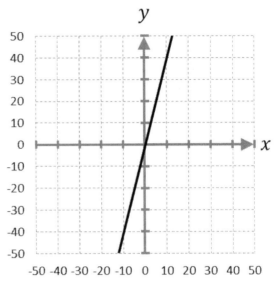

#5. y-intercept = _____

#6. y-intercept = _____

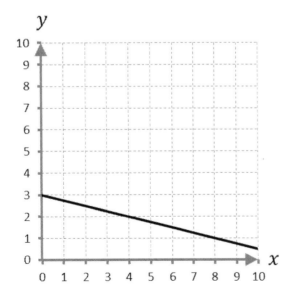

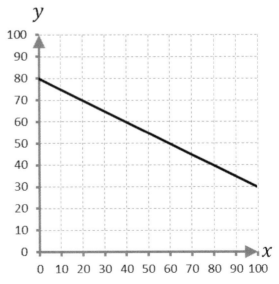

#7. y-intercept = _____

#8. y-intercept = _____

Determine the y-intercept of each line.

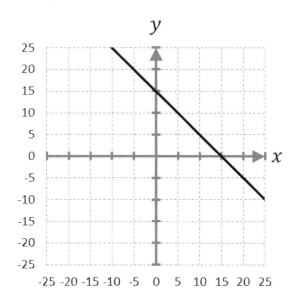 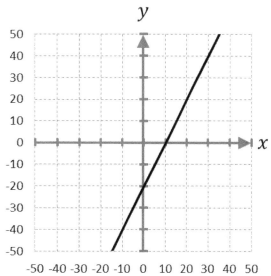

#9. y-intercept = _____   #10. y-intercept = _____

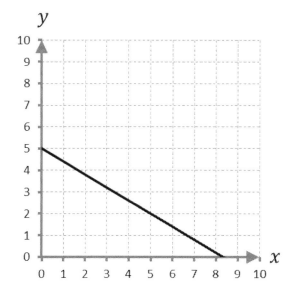 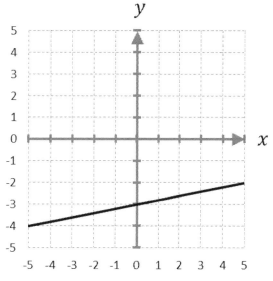

#11. y-intercept = _____   #12. y-intercept = _____

Determine the *y*-intercept of each line.

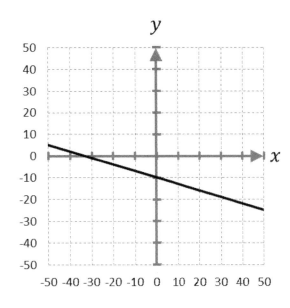

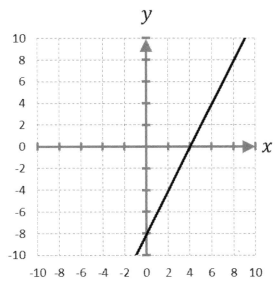

#13. *y*-intercept = _____   #14. *y*-intercept = _____

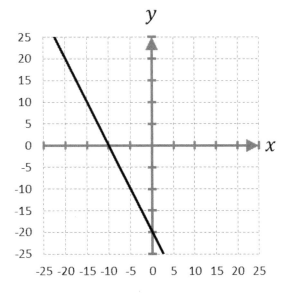

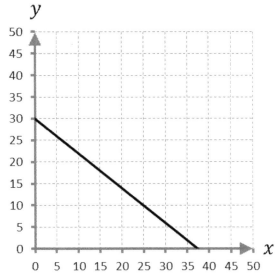

#15. *y*-intercept = _____   #16. *y*-intercept = _____

Chapter 8

Interpret the Equation for a Straight Line

Concepts

The equation for a straight line is:

$$y = mx + b$$

In this equation:
- m represents the slope
- b represents the y-intercept

Given an equation in slope-intercept form, it's easy to identify the slope and y-intercept:
- The slope, m, is the coefficient of x.
- The y-intercept, b, is the constant added to mx.

If the equation isn't already in the form $y = mx + b$, you must first use algebra to isolate y before identifying the slope and y-intercept.

These techniques are illustrated in the following examples.

Examples

Ex. 1. For the equation $y = 3x - 4$, find the slope and y-intercept.

This equation is already in slope-intercept form because it has the same structure as $y = mx + b$.

The slope, m, is the coefficient of x. Since 3 is multiplying x, the slope equals 3.

The y-intercept, b, is the constant added to mx. This constant is equal to –4.

$$m = 3 \text{ and } b = -4$$

Ex. 2. For the equation $2x - y = -3$, find the slope and y-intercept.

This equation is not in slope-intercept form, so we must first isolate y using algebra. This means to get y all by itself on one side.

First, add y to both sides to get

$$2x = -3 + y$$

Now add 3 to both sides:

$$y = 2x + 3$$

> Note that
> $2x + 3 = y$
> is the same as
> $y = 2x + 3$.

Once the equation is in slope-intercept form, identify m and b:

$$m = 2 \text{ and } b = 3$$

Ex. 3. For the equation $3y = 6x + 9$, find the slope and y-intercept.

This equation is not in slope-intercept form, so we must first isolate y using algebra. This means to get y all by itself on one side.

Divide both sides by 3 to isolate y:

$$y = \frac{6x + 9}{3} = \frac{6x}{3} + \frac{9}{3} = 2x + 3$$

Identify m and b in the equation $y = 2x + 3$:

$$m = 2 \text{ and } b = 3$$

Ex. 4. For the equation $2y - 4 = -2x$, find the slope and y-intercept.

This equation is not in slope-intercept form, so we must first isolate y using algebra. This means to get y all by itself on one side.

First, add 4 to both sides to get

$$2y = -2x + 4$$

Now divide both sides by 2:

$$y = \frac{-2x + 4}{2} = \frac{-2x}{2} + \frac{4}{2} = -x + 2$$

Identify m and b in the equation $y = -x + 2$:

$$m = -1 \text{ and } b = 2$$

The coefficient of $-x$ is -1.

Determine the slope and y-intercept from the equation of each line.

#1. $y = 8x + 5$

#2. $x + y = 4$

$m =$ _____ and $b =$ _____

$m =$ _____ and $b =$ _____

#3. $y = 2 + 3x$

#4. $2y = 4x + 8$

$m =$ _____ and $b =$ _____

$m =$ _____ and $b =$ _____

Determine the slope and y-intercept from the equation of each line.

#5. $\quad y = -6x + 1$

#6. $\quad 2 - y = -x$

$m =$ _____ and $b =$ _____ $\qquad m =$ _____ and $b =$ _____

#7. $\quad 3y - 9x = -6$

#8. $\quad 3x - 4 = y$

$m =$ _____ and $b =$ _____ $\qquad m =$ _____ and $b =$ _____

Determine the slope and y-intercept from the equation of each line.

#9. $y = -x - 1$ #10. $y = -3x$

$m =$ _____ and $b =$ _____ $m =$ _____ and $b =$ _____

#11. $-y = 2x + 7$ #12. $8 - 8x = 4y$

$m =$ _____ and $b =$ _____ $m =$ _____ and $b =$ _____

Determine the slope and y-intercept from the equation of each line.

#13. $5y - 5x = 10$ #14. $x - 2 = -y$

$m =$ _____ and $b =$ _____ $m =$ _____ and $b =$ _____

#15. $2y = -8x - 6$ #16. $y = -5$

$m =$ _____ and $b =$ _____ $m =$ _____ and $b =$ _____

Determine the slope and y-intercept from the equation of each line.

#17. $-y = -5x - 3$ #18. $6 = y$

$m = $ _____ and $b = $ _____ $m = $ _____ and $b = $ _____

#19. $y - 3 = 5 - x$ #20. $x = 2y$

$m = $ _____ and $b = $ _____ $m = $ _____ and $b = $ _____

Chapter 9

Write the Equation for a Straight Line

Concepts

Given a graph of a straight line, you can determine the equation for the line as follows:

- First, find the slope following the technique of Chapter 6.
- Next, find the y-intercept as described in Chapter 7.
- Finally, put these in the form $y = mx + b$, as shown in Chapter 8.

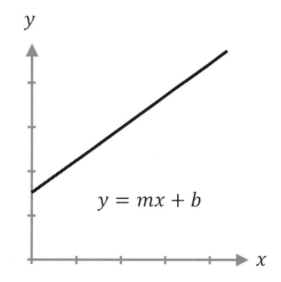

Example

Ex. 1. Write the equation for the line shown in the graph.

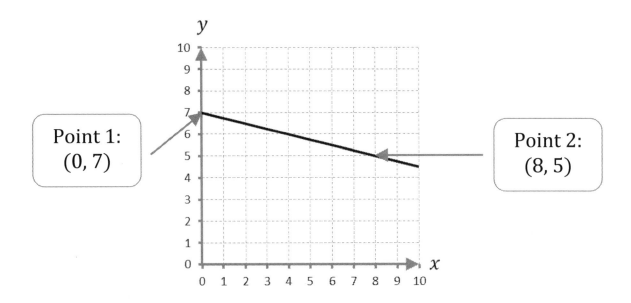

Point 1: $(0, 7)$

Point 2: $(8, 5)$

Read the (x, y) coordinates of two different points on the line:
- $(x_1, y_1) = (0, 7)$
- $(x_2, y_2) = (8, 5)$

Plug these points into the slope formula from Chapter 5:

$$m = \frac{y_2 - y_1}{x_2 - x_1} = \frac{5 - 7}{8 - 0} = \frac{-2}{8} = -\frac{1}{4} = -0.25$$

Identify the y-intercept as shown in Chapter 7: $b = 7$.

Insert m and b into the equation $y = mx + b$, as described in Chapter 8:

$$y = -0.25x + 7$$

#1. Write the equation for the line shown in the graph.

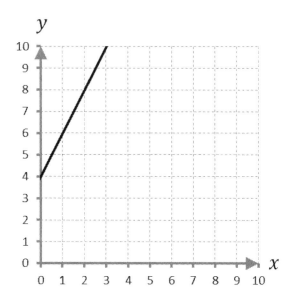

Mark the two points above that you are using to find the slope.

Show your work here:

$m =$ _____ and $b =$ _____

Write the equation here: _____

#2. Write the equation for the line shown in the graph.

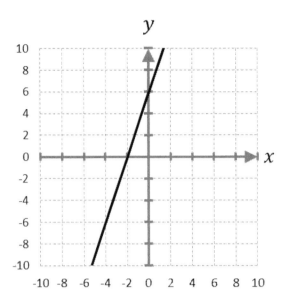

Mark the two points above that you are using to find the slope.

Show your work here:

$m =$ _____ and $b =$ _____

Write the equation here: _____

#3. Write the equation for the line shown in the graph.

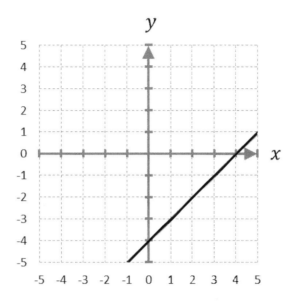

Mark the two points above that you are using to find the slope.

Show your work here:

$m =$ _____ and $b =$ _____

Write the equation here: _____

x 83 y

#4. Write the equation for the line shown in the graph.

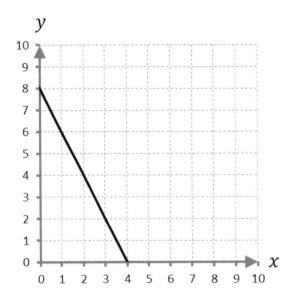

Mark the two points above that you are using to find the slope.

Show your work here:

$m =$ _____ and $b =$ _____

Write the equation here: _____

#5. Write the equation for the line shown in the graph.

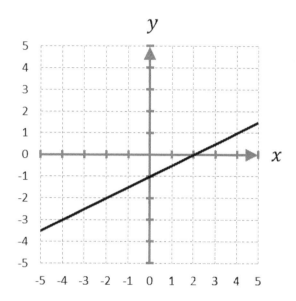

Mark the two points above that you are using to find the slope.

Show your work here:

$m =$ _____ and $b =$ _____

Write the equation here: _____

#6. Write the equation for the line shown in the graph.

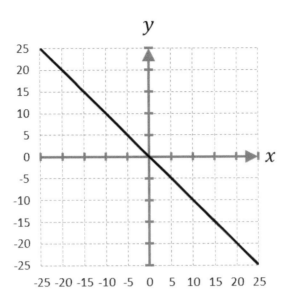

Mark the two points above that you are using to find the slope.

Show your work here:

$m =$ _____ and $b =$ _____

Write the equation here: _____

#7. Write the equation for the line shown in the graph.

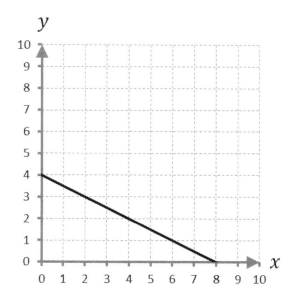

Mark the two points above that you are using to find the slope.

Show your work here:

$m =$ _____ and $b =$ _____

Write the equation here: _____

#8. Write the equation for the line shown in the graph.

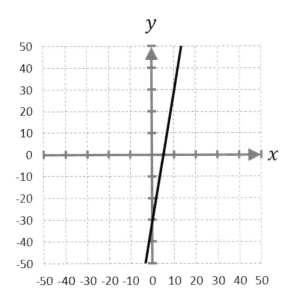

Mark the two points above that you are using to find the slope.

Show your work here:

$m =$ _____ and $b =$ _____

Write the equation here: _____

#9. Write the equation for the line shown in the graph.

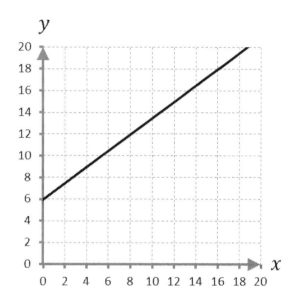

Mark the two points above that you are using to find the slope.

Show your work here:

$m =$ _____ and $b =$ _____

Write the equation here: _____

#10. Write the equation for the line shown in the graph.

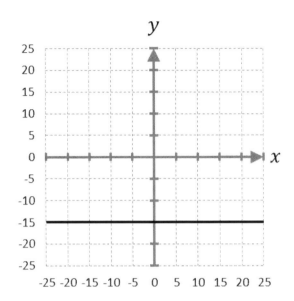

Mark the two points above that you are using to find the slope.

Show your work here:

$m =$ _____ and $b =$ _____

Write the equation here: _____

#11. Write the equation for the line shown in the graph.

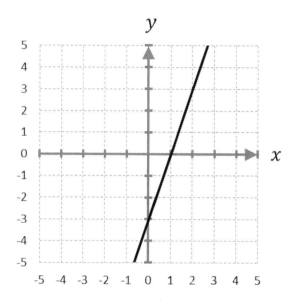

Mark the two points above that you are using to find the slope.

Show your work here:

$m =$ _____ and $b =$ _____

Write the equation here: _____

x 91 y

#12. Write the equation for the line shown in the graph.

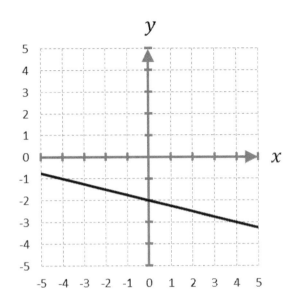

Mark the two points above that you are using to find the slope.

Show your work here:

$m =$ _____ and $b =$ _____

Write the equation here: _____

#13. Write the equation for the line shown in the graph.

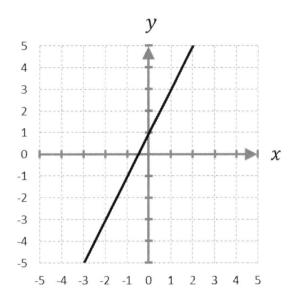

Mark the two points above that you are using to find the slope.

Show your work here:

$m = $ _____ and $b = $ _____

Write the equation here: _____

#14. Write the equation for the line shown in the graph.

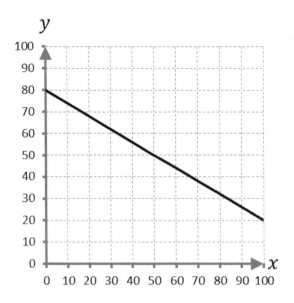

Mark the two points above that you are using to find the slope.

Show your work here:

$m =$ _____ and $b =$ _____

Write the equation here: _____

#15. Write the equation for the line shown in the graph.

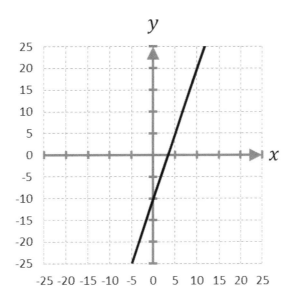

Mark the two points above that you are using to find the slope.

Show your work here:

$m =$ _____ and $b =$ _____

Write the equation here: _____

#16. Find the slope of the line shown in the graph.

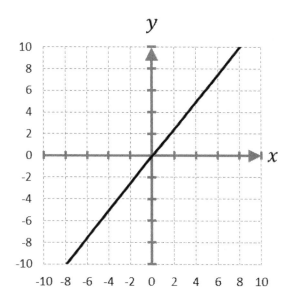

Mark the two points above that you are using to find the slope.

Show your work here:

$m =$ _____ and $b =$ _____

Write the equation here: _____

Chapter 10

Draw a Line Given the Equation

Concepts

Given the equation for a straight line in the form $y = mx + b$, you can graph the line following these steps:

- First, use the value of b to mark the y-intercept. The line must pass through the point $(0, b)$.
- Next, plug a nonzero value of x into $y = mx + b$ and solve for y. The line must pass through this point (x, y). Draw a straight line connecting these two points with a ruler.

Take a moment to check your answer:

- Check the sign of m. If m is positive, the line slopes up to the right. If m is negative, the line slopes down to the right.
- Plug another value of x into $y = mx + b$ and solve for y. The line must also pass through these (x, y) coordinates.

Note two special cases.

- If the line has the form $y = b$ (i.e. there is no x term), the line is horizontal.
- If the line has the form $x = a$ (i.e. there is no y term), the line is vertical.

This strategy is illustrated in the following examples.

Examples

Ex. 1. Graph the equation $y = 2x - 3$. Use a ruler.

Comparing $y = 2x - 3$ to $y = mx + b$, we see that the y-intercept is $b = -3$. One point is $(0, -3)$.

Plugging $x = 2$ into the equation $y = 2x - 3$ gives

$$y = 2x - 3 = 2(2) - 3 = 4 - 3 = 1$$

This point is $(2, 1)$. Draw a straight line through $(0, -3)$ and $(2, 1)$.

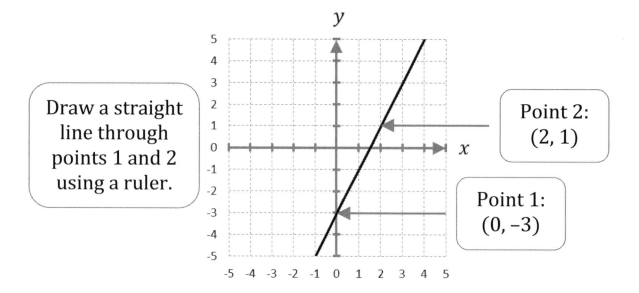

Draw a straight line through points 1 and 2 using a ruler.

Point 2: $(2, 1)$

Point 1: $(0, -3)$

Check your answer:
- The slope, $m = 2$, is positive. The line should slope up to the right, and it does.
- Plug in another point. Let's choose $x = 4$.
  $$y = 2x - 3 = 2(4) - 3 = 8 - 3 = 5$$
- The line does pass through the point $(4, 5)$.

Ex. 2. Graph the equation $y = -x + 5$. Use a ruler.

Comparing $y = -x + 5$ to $y = mx + b$, we see that the y-intercept is $b = 5$. One point is $(0, 5)$.

Plugging $x = 2$ into the equation $y = -x + 5$ gives

$$y = -x + 5 = -2 + 5 = 3$$

This point is $(2, 3)$. Draw a straight line through $(0, 5)$ and $(2, 3)$.

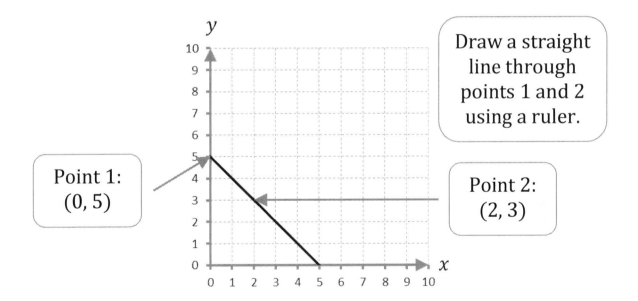

Point 1: $(0, 5)$

Draw a straight line through points 1 and 2 using a ruler.

Point 2: $(2, 3)$

Check your answer:
- The slope, $m = -1$, is negative. The line should slope down to the right, and it does.
- Plug in another point. Let's choose $x = 4$.
$$y = -x + 5 = -4 + 5 = 1$$
- The line does pass through the point $(4, 1)$.

#1. Graph the equation $y = x + 2$. Use a ruler.

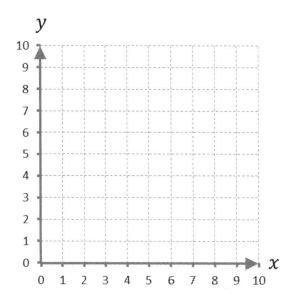

Show your calculations in this space:

List the (x, y) coordinates of points 1 and 2 here:

$$(x_1, y_1) = \underline{\hspace{2cm}} \quad (x_2, y_2) = \underline{\hspace{2cm}}$$

Need a little help? Try these suggested values:
- Solve for y at $x = 0$ and solve for y at $x = 4$.
- Check your answer at $x = 8$.

#2. Graph the equation $y = -2x + 4$. Use a ruler.

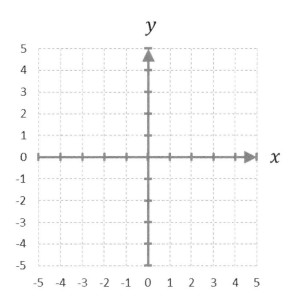

Show your calculations in this space:

List the (x, y) coordinates of points 1 and 2 here:

$$(x_1, y_1) = \underline{\hspace{2cm}} \qquad (x_2, y_2) = \underline{\hspace{2cm}}$$

Need a little help? Try these suggested values:
- Solve for y at $x = 0$ and solve for y at $x = 2$.
- Check your answer at $x = 4$.

#3. Graph the equation $y = 0.5x - 3$. Use a ruler.

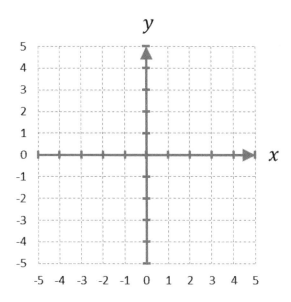

Show your calculations in this space:

List the (x, y) coordinates of points 1 and 2 here:

$$(x_1, y_1) = \underline{\hspace{2cm}} \quad (x_2, y_2) = \underline{\hspace{2cm}}$$

Need a little help? Try these suggested values:
- Solve for y at $x = 0$ and solve for y at $x = 2$.
- Check your answer at $x = 4$.

#4. Graph the equation $y = -x + 7$. Use a ruler.

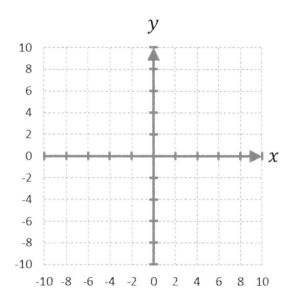

Show your calculations in this space:

List the (x, y) coordinates of points 1 and 2 here:

$$(x_1, y_1) = \underline{\hspace{2cm}} \quad (x_2, y_2) = \underline{\hspace{2cm}}$$

Need a little help? Try these suggested values:
- Solve for y at $x = 0$ and solve for y at $x = 4$.
- Check your answer at $x = 8$.

#5. Graph the equation $y = 2$. Use a ruler.

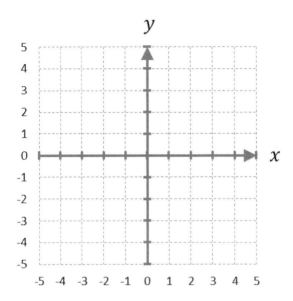

Show your calculations in this space:

List the (x, y) coordinates of points 1 and 2 here:

$$(x_1, y_1) = \underline{\hspace{2cm}} \quad (x_2, y_2) = \underline{\hspace{2cm}}$$

Need a little help? Try these suggested values:
- The value of y is the same regardless of x.
- What kind of line has zero slope?

#6. Graph the equation $y = 3x + 1$. Use a ruler.

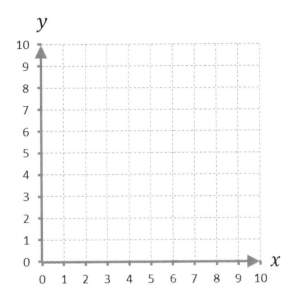

Show your calculations in this space:

List the (x, y) coordinates of points 1 and 2 here:

$$(x_1, y_1) = \underline{\hspace{2cm}} \quad (x_2, y_2) = \underline{\hspace{2cm}}$$

Need a little help? Try these suggested values:
- Solve for y at $x = 0$ and solve for y at $x = 2$.
- Check your answer at $x = 1$.

#7. Graph the equation $y = x$. Use a ruler.

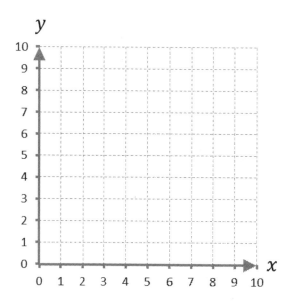

Show your calculations in this space:

List the (x, y) coordinates of points 1 and 2 here:

$(x_1, y_1) =$ _____ $(x_2, y_2) =$ _____

Need a little help? Try these suggested values:
- Solve for y at $x = 0$ and solve for y at $x = 5$.
- Check your answer at $x = 10$.

#8. Graph the equation $y = 0.25x + 8$. Use a ruler.

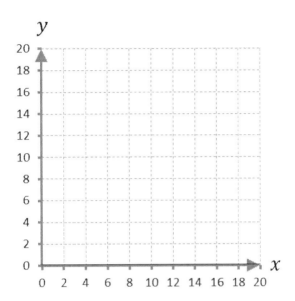

Show your calculations in this space:

List the (x, y) coordinates of points 1 and 2 here:

$$(x_1, y_1) = \underline{\hspace{2cm}} \quad (x_2, y_2) = \underline{\hspace{2cm}}$$

Need a little help? Try these suggested values:
- Solve for y at $x = 0$ and solve for y at $x = 8$.
- Check your answer at $x = 16$.

#9. Graph the equation $y = -0.5x - 1$. Use a ruler.

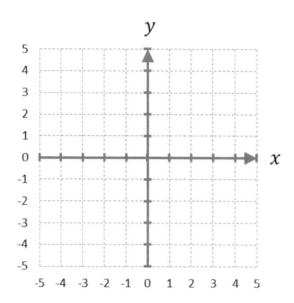

Show your calculations in this space:

List the (x, y) coordinates of points 1 and 2 here:

$$(x_1, y_1) = \underline{\hspace{2cm}} \quad (x_2, y_2) = \underline{\hspace{2cm}}$$

Need a little help? Try these suggested values:
- Solve for y at $x = 0$ and solve for y at $x = 2$.
- Check your answer at $x = 4$.

#10. Graph the equation $y = -2x + 20$. Use a ruler.

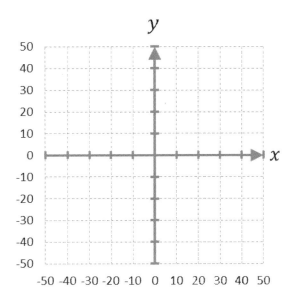

Show your calculations in this space:

List the (x, y) coordinates of points 1 and 2 here:

$$(x_1, y_1) = \underline{\hspace{2cm}} \quad (x_2, y_2) = \underline{\hspace{2cm}}$$

Need a little help? Try these suggested values:
- Solve for y at $x = 0$ and solve for y at $x = 10$.
- Check your answer at $x = 20$.

#11. Graph the equation $y = -x$. Use a ruler.

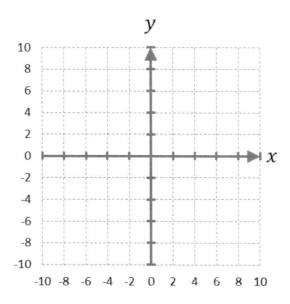

Show your calculations in this space:

List the (x, y) coordinates of points 1 and 2 here:

$$(x_1, y_1) = \underline{\hspace{2cm}} \quad (x_2, y_2) = \underline{\hspace{2cm}}$$

Need a little help? Try these suggested values:
- Solve for y at $x = 0$ and solve for y at $x = 4$.
- Check your answer at $x = 8$.

#12. Graph the equation $y = -0.5x + 14$. Use a ruler.

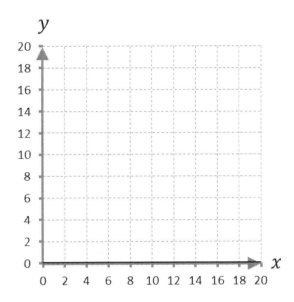

Show your calculations in this space:

List the (x, y) coordinates of points 1 and 2 here:

$$(x_1, y_1) = \underline{\hspace{2cm}} \quad (x_2, y_2) = \underline{\hspace{2cm}}$$

Need a little help? Try these suggested values:
- Solve for y at $x = 0$ and solve for y at $x = 8$.
- Check your answer at $x = 16$.

#13. Graph the equation $y = 2x + 30$. Use a ruler.

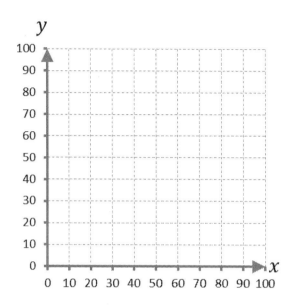

Show your calculations in this space:

List the (x, y) coordinates of points 1 and 2 here:

$$(x_1, y_1) = \underline{\hspace{2cm}} \quad (x_2, y_2) = \underline{\hspace{2cm}}$$

Need a little help? Try these suggested values:
- Solve for y at $x = 0$ and solve for y at $x = 10$.
- Check your answer at $x = 20$.

#14. Graph the equation $y = -3x - 15$. Use a ruler.

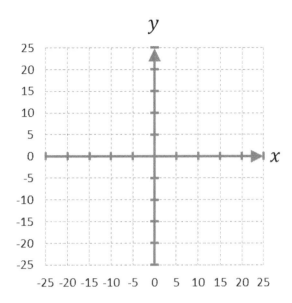

Show your calculations in this space:

List the (x, y) coordinates of points 1 and 2 here:

$(x_1, y_1) =$ _____ $(x_2, y_2) =$ _____

Need a little help? Try these suggested values:
- Solve for y at $x = 0$ and solve for y at $x = -5$.
- Check your answer at $x = -10$.

#15. Graph the equation $y = 0.8x - 20$. Use a ruler.

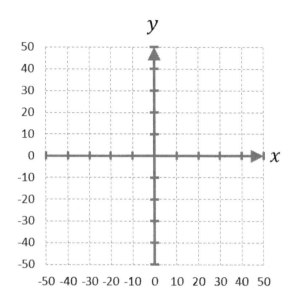

Show your calculations in this space:

List the (x, y) coordinates of points 1 and 2 here:

$$(x_1, y_1) = \text{_____} \quad (x_2, y_2) = \text{_____}$$

Need a little help? Try these suggested values:
- Solve for y at $x = 0$ and solve for y at $x = 50$.
- Check your answer at $x = 25$.

Chapter 11

Alternative Equation for a Straight Line

Concepts

The equation $y = mx + b$ that we have used in previous chapters is called slope-intercept form. This form of the equation makes it easy to identify the slope and y-intercept.

One alternative to the slope-intercept form is called the point-slope form. Point-slope form has the following structure:

$$y - y_1 = m(x - x_1)$$

In this equation:
- m represents the slope of the line.
- (x_1, y_1) are the coordinates of any point on the line.

Point-slope form is convenient when you know the slope and a point on the line. Slope-intercept form is convenient when you know the slope and y-intercept.

Given point-slope form, you can find the slope-intercept form using algebra to isolate y.

Examples

Ex. 1. A line with a slope of 4 passes through the point (2, 1). Find the y-intercept.

First express the line in point-slope form. The slope is $m = 4$ and one point one the line has $x_1 = 2$, and $y_1 = 1$.

Plug these values into the equation for point-slope form:

$$y - y_1 = m(x - x_1)$$
$$y - 1 = 4(x - 2)$$

Use algebra to isolate y. Distribute the 4:

$$y - 1 = 4x - 8$$

Add 1 to both sides:

$$y = 4x - 8 + 1$$
$$y = 4x - 7$$

This equation has slope-intercept form. Compare $y = 4x - 7$ to $y = mx + b$ to see that the y-intercept is:

$$b = -7$$

Check: See if the equation $y = 4x - 7$ agrees with the given point, (2, 1). Plug $x = 2$ into $y = 4x - 7$ and see if $y = 1$.

$$y = 4(2) - 7 = 8 - 7 = 1$$

Since $y = 1$, the equation checks out.

Ex. 2. A line with a slope of –3 passes through the point (4, –1). Find the y-intercept.

First express the line in point-slope form. The slope is $m = -3$ and one point one the line has $x_1 = 4$, and $y_1 = -1$.

Plug these values into the equation for point-slope form:

$$y - y_1 = m(x - x_1)$$
$$y - (-1) = -3(x - 4)$$

Use algebra to isolate y. Distribute the –3:

$$y + 1 = -3x + 12$$

(Recall that two minuses make a plus.) Subtract 1 from both sides:

$$y = -3x + 12 - 1$$
$$y = -3x + 11$$

This equation has slope-intercept form. Compare $y = -3x + 11$ to $y = mx + b$ to see that the y-intercept is:

$$b = 11$$

Check: See if the equation $y = -3x + 11$ agrees with the given point, $(4, -1)$. Plug $x = 4$ into $y = -3x + 11$ and see if $y = -1$.

$$y = -3(4) + 11 = -12 + 11 = -1$$

Since $y = -1$, the equation checks out.

#1. A line with a slope of 2 passes through the point (8, 2).
Find the *y*-intercept.

Show your work here:

Final answer = _____

#2. A line with a slope of –1 passes through the point (6, 2). Find the y-intercept.

Show your work here:

Final answer = _____

#3. A line with a slope of –7 passes through the origin.
Find the *y*-intercept.

Show your work here:

Final answer = _____

#4. A line with a slope of 3 passes through the point (1, 7). Find the y-intercept.

Show your work here:

Final answer = _____

#5. A line with a slope of 0.5 passes through the point (6, –8). Find the y-intercept.

Show your work here:

Final answer = _____

#6. A line with a slope of –2 passes through the point (–4, 1). Find the *y*-intercept.

Show your work here:

Final answer = _____

#7. A line with a slope of 1 passes through the point (9, 6). Find the y-intercept.

Show your work here:

Final answer = _____

#8. A line with a slope of 5 passes through the point (4, 0). Find the y-intercept.

Show your work here:

Final answer = _____

#9. A line with a slope of 0.25 passes through the point (20, 10). Find the y-intercept.

Show your work here:

Final answer = _____

#10. A line with a slope of –0.5 passes through the point (4, 8). Find the *y*-intercept.

Show your work here:

Final answer = _____

#11. A line with a slope of –2 passes through the point (3, –6). Find the *y*-intercept.

Show your work here:

Final answer = _____

#12. A line with a slope of 4 passes through the point $(-2, 8)$. Find the y-intercept.

Show your work here:

Final answer = _____

#13. A line with a slope of –2 passes through the point (6, –3). Find the *y*-intercept.

Show your work here:

Final answer = _____

#14. A line with a slope of –3 passes through the point (6, 7). Find the y-intercept.

Show your work here:

Final answer = _____

#15. A line with a slope of 0.75 passes through the point (−8, −8). Find the *y*-intercept.

Show your work here:

Final answer = _____

Chapter 12

Challenge Problems

Concepts

The challenge of this chapter helps to build valuable skills:
- applying the same concepts in new ways
- reasoning through the solutions
- adapting to new situations
- learning how to solve a variety of problems

These skills are not easy to teach directly. However, these valuable skills can be developed through practice.

For Chapter 12, the answer key includes brief explanations to help you understand the solution. If you get stuck, read the explanation in the answer key, and then try to work out the solution.

No Examples

Chapter 12 doesn't include any examples.

The idea behind this chapter is to learn how to apply ideas to different situations.

- You can't learn this valuable skill by copying from an example of every possible situation.
- You learn this skill be trying (but, where necessary, consulting the explanations in the answer key and trying to solve the problem again).

Need Help?

If you're stuck, you can find explanations for Chapter 12 in the Answer Key at the back of the book.

You learn more by trying it yourself first, even if you feel unsure. Try something. It might be wrong, but that's okay. That's how you learn. Try it out first, then read the explanation.

But if you can't figure out how to get started, it's okay to read the explanation.

After you read the explanation, return to the problem and try to solve it. Check your answer at the back of the book.

Remember, every problem in every class is easy once you learn and understand how to solve it.

#1. Given the equation $y = 3x + 8$, what is the value of y when x equals 14?

Show your work here:

Final answer: _____

#2. Given the equation $y = 3x + 8$, what is the value of x when y equals 14? (Notice how this differs from Problem #1.)

Show your work here:

Final answer: _____

#3. A line with a slope of 2 passes through the point (4, 3).
Write the equation for the line in slope-intercept form.

Show your work here:

Final answer: _____

#4. A line passes through the points (6, 3) and (8, 9).
Write the equation for the line in slope-intercept form.

Show your work here:

Final answer: _____

#5. A line passes through the points (−2, 3) and (4, 12).
Find the y-intercept.

Show your work here:

Final answer: _____

#6. The equation for a line is $y = 2x + 6$. Find the x-intercept. (This is not the same thing as the y-intercept. However, x-intercept is defined the same way as y-intercept is defined. This is enough information to figure this out, but if you would like help, see the explanation given in the answer key.)

Show your work here:

Final answer: _____

#7. A line passes through the points (3, 4) and (6, 10).
Find the x-intercept. (See the note in the previous exercise.)

Show your work here:

Final answer: _____

#8. A line with a y-intercept of 4 passes through the point (2, 8). Find the slope.

Show your work here:

Final answer: _____

#9. A line with a y-intercept of –2 passes through the point (1, –10). Write the equation for the line in slope-intercept form.

Show your work here:

Final answer: _____

#10. Determine the y-intercept of the line graphed below.

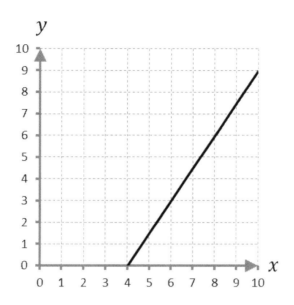

Show your work here:

Final answer: _____

#11. Determine the equation for the line graphed below.

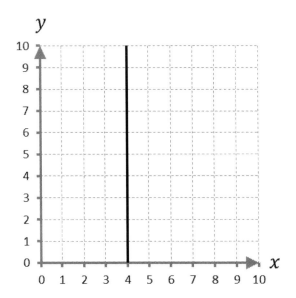

Show your work here:

Final answer: _____

#12. Graph the equation $2x = 4y - 8$.

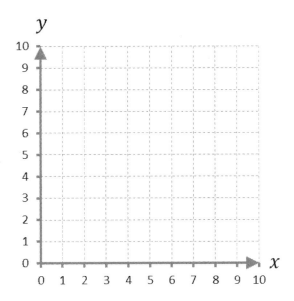

Show your work here:

#13. Graph the equation $x = -3$.

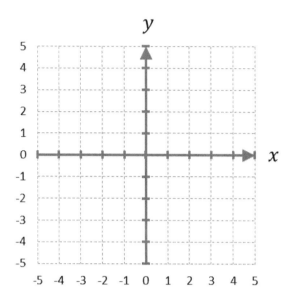

Show your work here:

#14. Graph the equation $y = -2x + 70$.

This graph doesn't have its own numerical scale to begin with.

You must first choose a numerical scale and draw this on the graph before you draw the line on the graph.

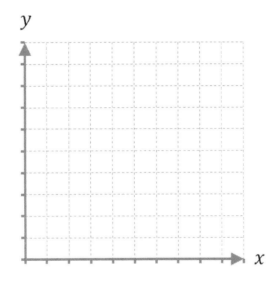

Show your work here:

#15. Graph the equation $y = -0.4x - 25$.

This graph doesn't have its own numerical scale to begin with.

You must first choose a numerical scale and draw this on the graph before you draw the line on the graph.

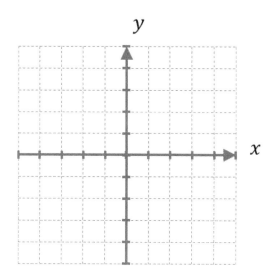

Show your work here:

Answer Key

Chapter 1

#1. (6, 9)   #2. (8, 2)

#3. (3, 4)   #4. (2, 1)

#5. (1, 7)   #6. (5, 3)

#7. (15, 20)   #8. (0, 3)

#9. (7, 5)   #10. (2, 0)

#11. (4.5, 1.5)   #12. (12.5, 20)

#13. (80, 60)   #14. (25, 45)

#15. (0.6, 0.3)   #16. (0.3, 0.9)

Chapter 2

#1. (4, –3) #2. (–2, 5)

#3. (1, 3) #4. (–3, –5)

#5. (–4, 8) #6. (–9, –5)

#7. (0, –6) #8. (2, –7)

#9. (30, 20) #10. (–20, 0)

#11. (–70, –50) #12. (0.75, –0.75)

#13. (–50, –80) #14. (40, –10)

#15. (–17.5, 12.5) #16. (–0.25, 1)

Chapter 3

#1

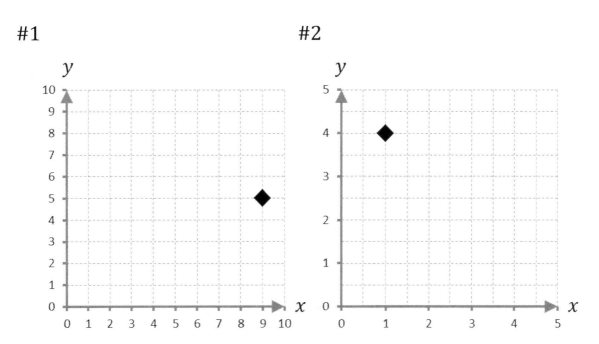

#2

#3

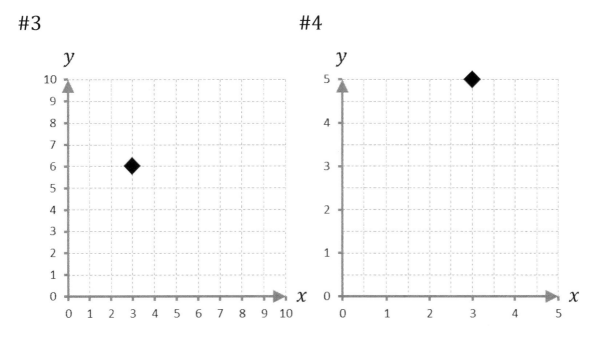

#4

#5

#6

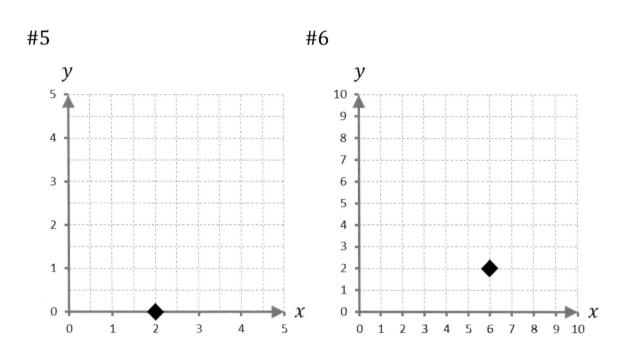

#7

#8

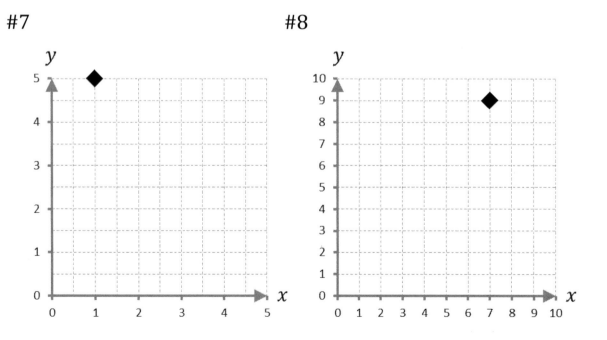

#9

#10

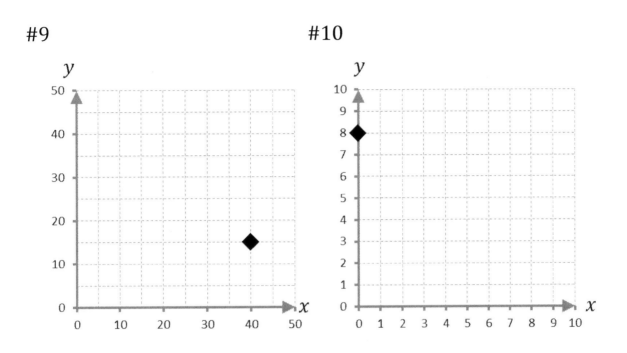

#11

#12

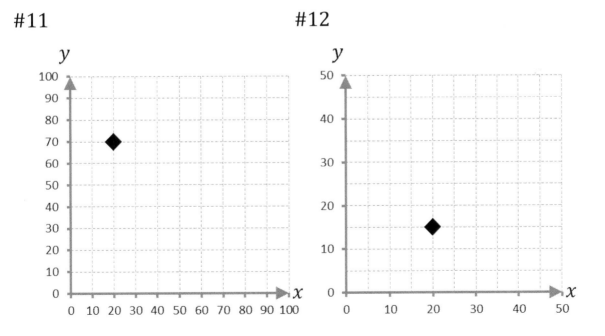

#13

#14

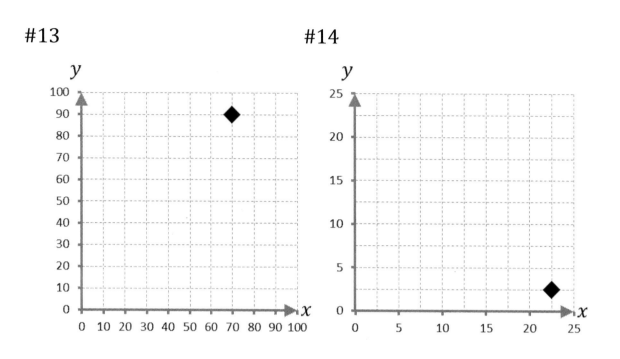

#15

#16

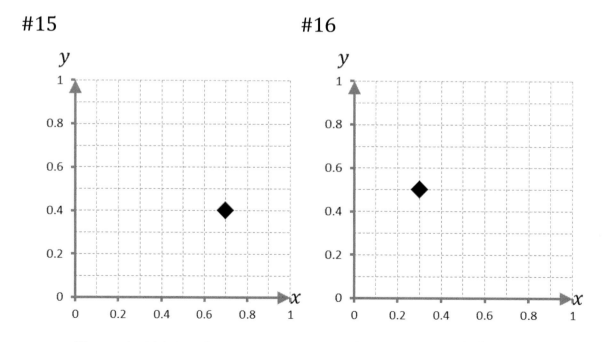

Chapter 4

#1

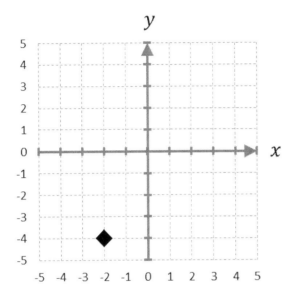

#2

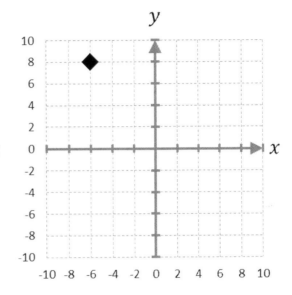

#3

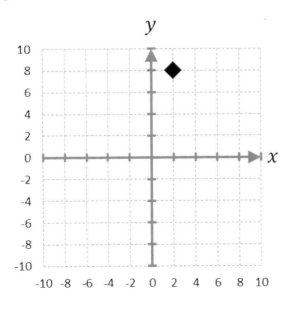

#4

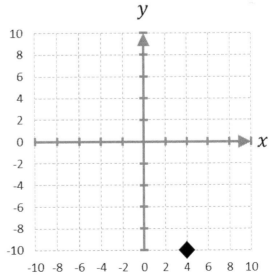

#5

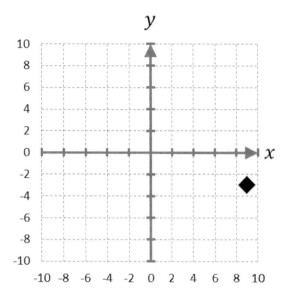

#6

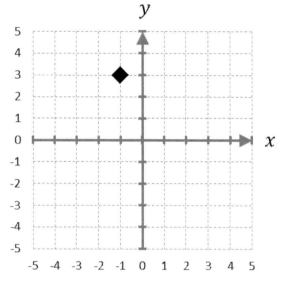

#7

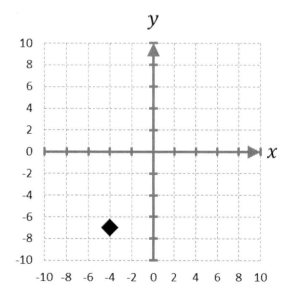

#8

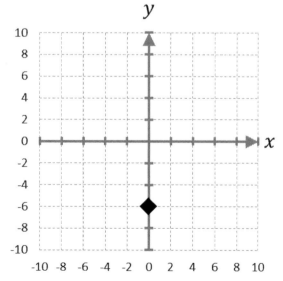

#9

#10

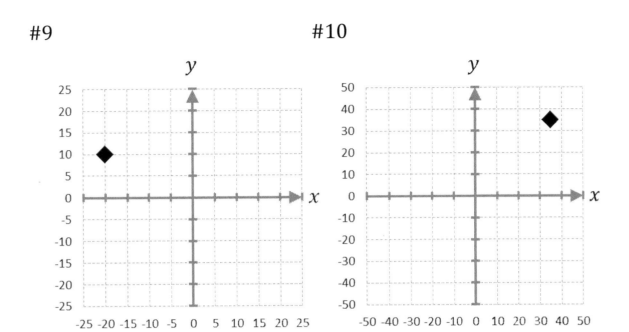

#11

#12

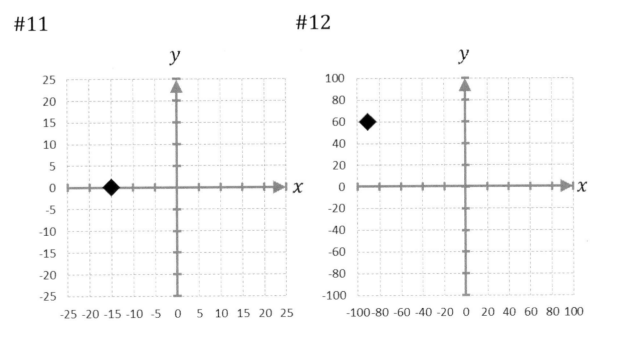

#13

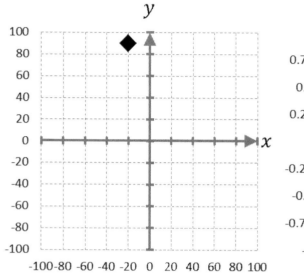

#14

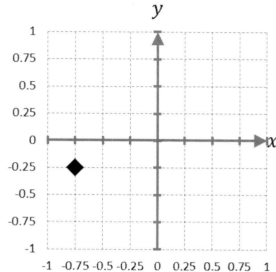

#15

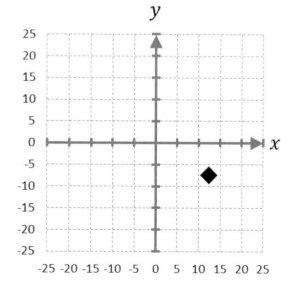

#16

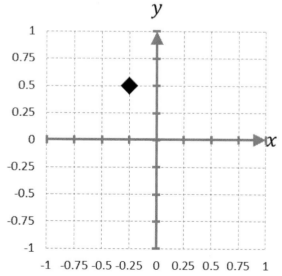

Chapter 5

#1. slope = 2 #2. slope = 6

#3. slope = 1 #4. slope = 0

#5. slope = 4 #6. slope = −2

#7. slope = 4 #8. slope = 2

#9. slope = −5 #10. slope = 3

#11. slope = −4 #12. slope = −9

#13. slope = 8 #14. slope = 2

#15. slope = −2 #16. slope = −3

Chapter 6

#1. slope = 2   #2. slope = 0.25

#3. slope = 3   #4. slope = −0.5

#5. slope = 1   #6. slope = −4

#7. slope = 0.75   #8. slope = −5

#9. slope = 0   #10. slope = 1.5

#11. slope = −8   #12. slope = 2.5

#13. slope = 6   #14. slope = −1.25

#15. slope = 0.4

Chapter 7

#1. y-intercept = 4   #2. y-intercept = 1

#3. y-intercept = 8   #4. y-intercept = −2

#5. y-intercept = −5   #6. y-intercept = 0

#7. y-intercept = 3   #8. y-intercept = 80

#9. y-intercept = 15   #10. y-intercept = −20

#11. y-intercept = 5   #12. y-intercept = −3

#13. y-intercept = −10   #14. y-intercept = −8

#15. y-intercept = −20   #16. y-intercept = 30

Chapter 8

#1. $m = 8$ and $b = 5$

#2. $m = -1$ and $b = 4$

#3. $m = 3$ and $b = 2$

#4. $m = 2$ and $b = 4$

#5. $m = -6$ and $b = 1$

#6. $m = 1$ and $b = 2$

#7. $m = 3$ and $b = -2$

#8. $m = 3$ and $b = -4$

#9. $m = -1$ and $b = -1$

#10. $m = -3$ and $b = 0$

#11. $m = -2$ and $b = -7$

#12. $m = -2$ and $b = 2$

#13. $m = 1$ and $b = 2$

#14. $m = -1$ and $b = 2$

#15. $m = -4$ and $b = -3$

#16. $m = 0$ and $b = -5$

#17. $m = 5$ and $b = 3$

#18. $m = 0$ and $b = 6$

#19. $m = -1$ and $b = 8$

#20. $m = 0.5$ and $b = 0$

Chapter 9

#1. $y = 2x + 4$

#2. $y = 3x + 6$

#3. $y = x - 4$

#4. $y = -2x + 8$

#5. $y = 0.5x - 1$

#6. $y = -x$

#7. $y = -0.5x + 4$

#8. $y = 6x - 30$

#9. $y = 0.75x + 6$

#10. $y = -15$

#11. $y = 3x - 3$

#12. $y = -0.25x - 2$

#13. $y = 2x + 1$

#14. $y = -0.6x + 80$

#15. $y = 3x - 10$

#16. $y = 1.25x$

Chapter 10

#1

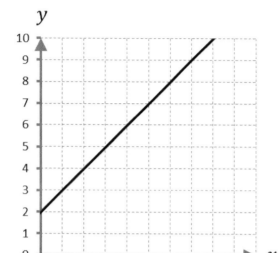

#2

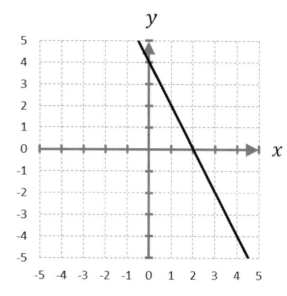

#3

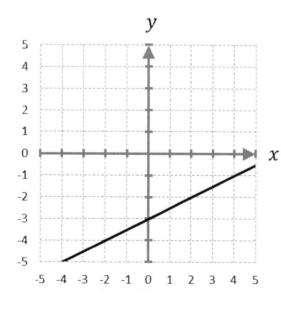

#4

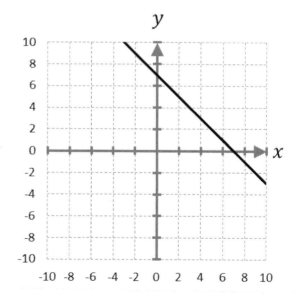

#5

#6

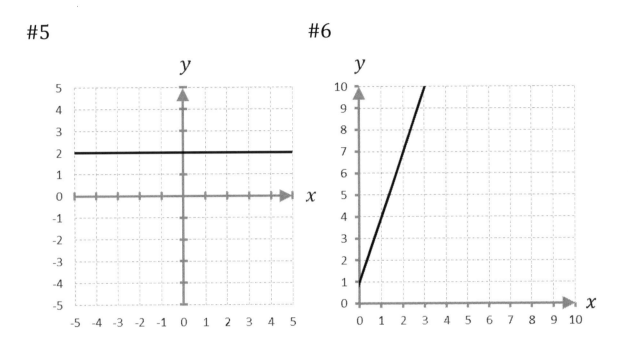

#7

#8

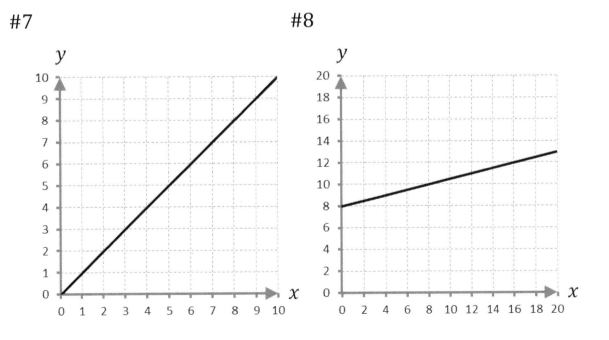

#9

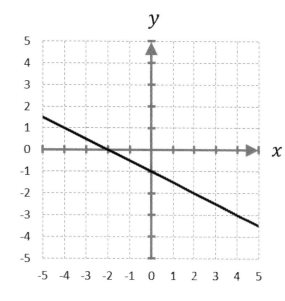

#10

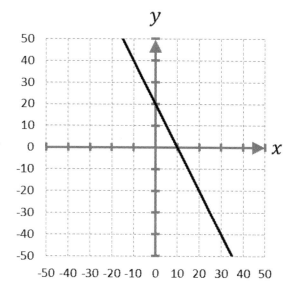

#11

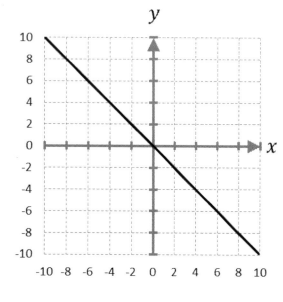

#12

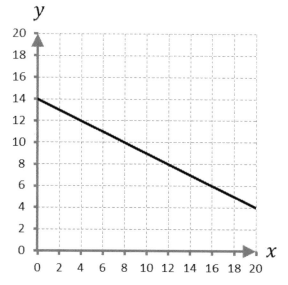

#13

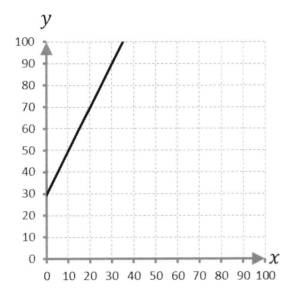

#14

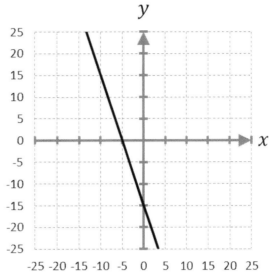

#15

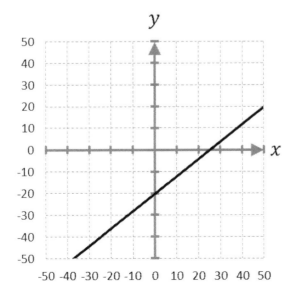

Chapter 11

#1. y–intercept $= -14$ #2. y–intercept $= 8$

#3. y–intercept $= 0$ #4. y–intercept $= 4$

#5. y–intercept $= -11$ #6. y–intercept $= -7$

#7. y–intercept $= -3$ #8. y–intercept $= -20$

#9. y–intercept $= 5$ #10. y–intercept $= 10$

#11. y–intercept $= 0$ #12. y–intercept $= 16$

#13. y–intercept $= 9$ #14. y–intercept $= 25$

#15. y–intercept $= -2$

Chapter 12

#1. $y = 50$

- Plug x into the given equation to find y.

#2. $x = 2$

- Plug y into the given equation.
- Then use algebra to isolate x.

#3. $y = 2x - 5$

- Follow the strategy from Chapter 11.

#4. $y = 3x - 15$

- Use the strategy from Chapter 5 to find the slope. You should find that $m = 3$.
- Then use the strategy from Chapter 11 (with one of the given points) to find the equation.

#5. $b = 6$

- Use the strategy from Chapter 5 to find the slope. You should find that $m = 1.5$.
- Then use the strategy from Chapter 11 (with one of the given points) to find the y-intercept.

#6. x-intercept $= -3$

- The x-intercept is the value of x when $y = 0$. You could figure this out knowing that the y-intercept is the value of y when $x = 0$ (see Chapter 7).
- Plug $y = 0$ into the given equation.
- Then use algebra to isolate x. You should get $x = -3$ when you plug in $y = 0$. The answer is -3.

#7. x-intercept $= 1$

- Use the strategy from Chapter 5 to find the slope. You should find that $m = 2$.
- Next use the strategy from Chapter 11 (with one of the given points) to find the slope-intercept equation. You should get $y = 2x - 2$.
- Plug $y = 0$ into the slope-intercept equation.
- Then use algebra to isolate x. You should get $x = 1$ when you plug in $y = 0$. The answer is 1.

#8. $m = 2$

- One point is $(0, 4)$ because $x = 0$ at the y-intercept.
- Use the points $(0, 4)$ and $(2, 8)$ with the strategy from Chapter 5 to find the slope.

#9. $y = -8x - 2$
- One point is $(0, -2)$ because $x = 0$ at the y-intercept.
- Use the points $(0, -2)$ and $(1, -10)$ with the strategy from Chapter 5 to find the slope. You should find that $m = -8$.
- Then plug the slope and y-intercept into the equation $y = mx + b$.

#10. $b = -6$
- First find the slope using the strategy from Chapter 6. You should find that $m = 1.5$.
- Next plug any point on the line into the equation $y = 1.5x + b$ and use algebra to isolate b. One point on the line is $(4, 0)$, so you could plug in $x = 4$ and $y = 0$.

#11. $x = 4$
- This problem is a little tricky. If you try to solve for the slope, what you get is undefined (because the run is zero).
- This means that you must approach the problem another way. Think about what's going on in the graph: The value of x isn't changing. No matter what y is, x equals 4. Therefore, the equation is $x = 4$.
- An alternative solution is to recall that an equation of the form $y = b$ produces a horizontal line. Similarly, an equation of the form $x = a$ produces a vertical line.

#12.

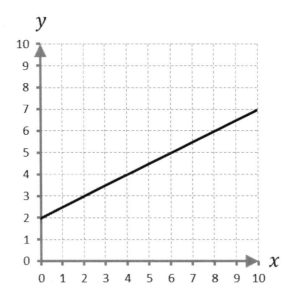

- First use algebra to isolate y.
- Then follow the strategy from Chapter 10.

#13.

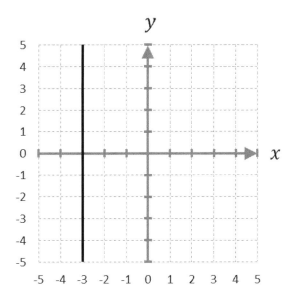

- This time, you can't use algebra to isolate y because the given equation doesn't have y in it.
- This problem is similar to Problem #11. See the explanation to Problem #11.
- Since $x = -3$ must be true for any value of y, the graph is a vertical line with $x = -3$.

#14.

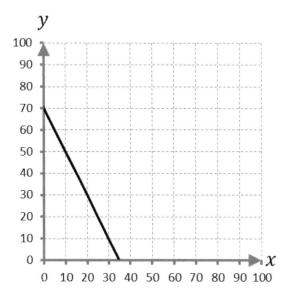

- Choose minimum and maximum values of x and y to label on the graph.
- The y-intercept is 70. If you choose $+100$ as the maximum and 0 as the minimum, this will leave enough room to draw the graph.
- Now follow the strategy from Chapter 10.

#15.

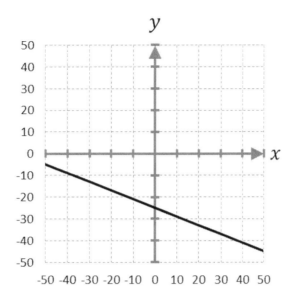

- Choose minimum and maximum values of x and y to label on the graph.
- The y-intercept is −25. If you choose −50 as the minimum and +50 as the maximum, this will leave enough room to draw the graph.
- Now follow the strategy from Chapter 10.

About the Author

Chris McMullen is a physics instructor at Northwestern State University of Louisiana and also an author of academic books. Whether in the classroom or as a writer, Dr. McMullen loves sharing knowledge and the art of motivating and engaging students.

He earned his Ph.D. in phenomenological high-energy physics (particle physics) from Oklahoma State University in 2002. Originally from California, Dr. McMullen earned his Master's degree in physics from California State University, Northridge, where his thesis was in the field of electron spin resonance.

As a physics teacher, Dr. McMullen observed that many students lack fluency in fundamental math skills. In an effort to help students of all ages and levels master basic math skills, he published a series of math workbooks on arithmetic, fractions, algebra, and trigonometry called the *Improve Your Math Fluency* series. Dr. McMullen has also published a variety of science books, including introductions to basic astronomy and chemistry concepts in addition to physics textbooks.

Dr. McMullen is very passionate about teaching. Many students and observers have been impressed with the transformation that occurs when he walks into the classroom, and the interactive engaged discussions that he leads during class time. Dr. McMullen is well-known for drawing monkeys and using them in his physics examples and problems, using his creativity to inspire students. A stressed out student is likely to be told to throw some bananas at monkeys, smile, and think happy physics thoughts.

Author, Chris McMullen, Ph.D.

Improve Your Math Fluency

This series of math workbooks is geared toward practicing essential math skills:

- Algebra
- Trigonometry
- Graphing
- Fractions, decimals, and percents
- Long division
- Multiplication and division
- Addition and subtraction

www.improveyourmathfluency.com

www.chrismcmullen.com

300+ Mathematical Pattern Puzzles

Chris McMullen enjoys solving puzzles. His favorite puzzle is Kakuro (kind of like a cross between crossword puzzles and Sudoku). He once taught a three-week summer course on puzzles.

If you enjoy mathematical pattern puzzles, you might appreciate:

Number Pattern Recognition & Reasoning
- pattern recognition
- visual discrimination
- analytical skills
- logic and reasoning
- analogies
- mathematics

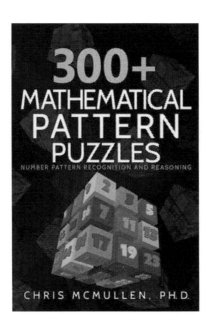

Printed in Great Britain
by Amazon